D0471427

THE BIG BOOK OF ONE DIRECTION

Mary Boone

This book is available in quantity at special discounts for your group or organization. For further information, contact:

Triumph Books LLC
814 North Franklin Street
Chicago, Illinois 60610
Phone: (312) 337-0747
www.triumphbooks.com

Printed in U.S.A.

ISBN: 978-1-60078-793-5

Content developed and packaged by Rockett Media, Inc.
Writer: Mary Boone
Editor: Bob Baker
Design and Page Production: Andrew Burwell
Cover Design by Andy Hansen

Photographs courtesy of Getty Images unless otherwise noted

THE BIG BOOK OF ONE DIRECTION

Chapter 1: Beautiful Beginnings

Chapter 2: Worldwide Success

Chapter 3: Cheeky Niall

Chapter 4: Vain Zayn

Chapter 5: Levelheaded Liam

Chapter 6: Harry the Ladies Man

Chapter 7: Louis the Prankster

Chapter 8: Directioners' Delight

Chapter 9: The Future Is Bright

Chapter 1:
BEAUTIFUL BEGINNINGS

Chapter 1:
BEAUTIFUL BEGINNINGS

One Direction is the band that almost wasn't.

These five individual guys – total strangers – auditioned for 2010's *The X Factor*. They made it through preliminary rounds but were cut at the boot camp stage of the competition.

Then – WHAM! BAM! – four girls along with Harry Styles, Liam Payne, Louis Tomlinson, Niall Horan and Zayn Malik were called back onto the stage.

Judges Simon Cowell, Louis Walsh and Nicole Scherzinger were willing to give these nine performers a second chance. The guys would perform together and the girls would perform together, and they could continue to compete as groups. Were they interested? Yes, of course they were. But –

•What if they hadn't been?

•What if they said, "We want to be solo stars – no group for us"?

•What if Harry or Louis or any of the other guys hadn't been offered that second chance?

•What if Liam had made it through to the competition when he auditioned for *The X Factor* two years earlier?

Just one misstep – one poorly performed song or super cranky judge – and One Direction might never have happened. But, to the relief of millions of fans worldwide, those "what ifs" are in the past and One Direction is very much in the present.

These handsome, talented young men are selling albums and concert tickets at record pace, showing up on the covers of fan magazines, and melting the hearts of girls and young women around the globe.

These five well-coiffed cuties may be the most famous "losers" that *The X Factor* has ever produced. The lifeline tossed to them on *The X Factor* has changed pop music in a very notable way.

In the beginning, the guys weren't even sure how to perform as a group. They were unfamiliar with harmonizing and meshing their ideas was a real challenge.

Thankfully, those anxieties subsided. The boys became quick friends and, with the aid of some intense rehearsal and coaching, they were able to sail through early competition and then onto the live shows, mentored by *The*

TUNED IN

The X Factor finale, during which One Direction came in third place, attracted an audience averaging 17.2 million viewers over its two-hour time slot. This was nearly 2 million viewers more than tuned in to watch the previous year's finale.

WINNERS

The X Factor *has produced eight UK winners to date: Steve Brookstein, Shayne Ward, Leona Lewis, Leon Jackson, Alexandra Burke, Joe McElderry, Matt Cardle and Little Mix.*

Chapter 1:
BEAUTIFUL BEGINNINGS

U.K. SENSATIONS

One Direction is certainly making its mark, but it has a way to go before becoming the best-selling U.K. act of all times. These acts rank tops worldwide, their names are followed by the total number of albums they've sold:

1. The Beatles, 248.8 million
2. Elton John, 153 million
3. Led Zeppelin, 133.4 million

* Sales figures include albums, singles, compilation-albums, music videos as well as downloads of singles and full-length albums.

X Factor creator Simon Cowell.

As the guys developed skills and confidence, they quickly attracted a huge fan base.

"Normally when you put together a band they have some time to go away and develop but we had to do that in a live competition, in front of 20 million people," says Liam. "If you make a mistake in front of an audience like that, you get voted out. We had no room for error whatsoever. We had to grow up very, very fast."

During the 10 weeks of live shows, One Direction covered songs ranging from Bryan Adams' "Summer of '69" and Coldplay's "Viva La Vida" to Kelly Clarkson's "My Life Would Suck Without You" and Snow Patrol's "Chasing Cars." Thanks to their very solid performances, they became the first manufactured group to make it through the show's first nine weeks of on-air competition.

In the show's final episode, the band performed Elton John's "Your Song," World Party's "She's the One" (with pop superstar Robbie Williams) and Natalie Imbruglia's "Torn."

Matt Cardle won *The X Factor* that year, followed by runner-up Rebecca Ferguson. One Direction's third place finish, however, has not harmed their career in any way.

In fact, on March 22, 2012, One Direction became the first UK group ever to debut at No. 1 on the U.S. Billboard 200 album chart, a feat they accomplished by knocking recording stars Bruce

THE X FACTOR

The X Factor originated in the United Kingdom. Versions of the show now air around the world, in places ranging from Armenia and China to the Czech Republic and the United States.

The "X Factor" in the show's title refers to that "special something" that makes an individual a star.

As of June 2012, there have been 70 winners of *The X Factor* from around the globe. One Direction is just one of the show's many success stories. Other former UK contestants who've made a splash include:

Shayne Ward

Shayne Ward won the 2005 series of the television talent show.

He released his first single, "That's My Goal," in December 2005. The song was available via download immediately after the show's finale and then in stores beginning Dec. 21, 2005; it sold more than 313,000 copies (including downloads) on its first day of release and became the fourth fastest selling UK single of all time. The single stayed on the charts until June 2006, selling more than 1.3 million copies.

His self-titled debut album was released in April 2006. It sold more than 200,000 in its first week of release in the UK, taking it straight to No. 1 on the UK album charts. Later on, the album was released worldwide; it has since been certified platinum.

In early 2007, Ward went on his first live tour across Ireland and the United Kingdom. He released his second album, *Breathless,* in November 2007. His third album, *Obsession,* was released in 2010.

In 2012, the singer could be found appearing as Stacee Jaxx in *Rock of Ages,* at Shaftesbury Theatre in London's West End.

JLS

JLS (short for Jack the Lad Swing) consists of members Aston Merrygold, Oritse Williams, JB Gill and Marvin Humes.

They were runners-up on the fifth season of *The X Factor.*

JLS's first two singles, "Beat Again" and "Everybody in Love," both went to No. 1 on the UK singles chart. The band's self-titled debut album was released in November 2009 and has since sold more than 1 million copies.

The band won awards for "British Breakthrough" and "British Single" at the 2010 BRIT Awards.

In 2010, JLS signed an American record deal with Jive Records and released "Everybody in Love" as their debut U.S. single.

As of June 2012, JLS has sold more than 3 million records.

Leona Lewis

Next to One Direction, Leona Lewis is arguably the biggest thing to come out of *The X Factor.* The 2006 champion has sold more than 10 million albums.

Lewis' debut album, *Spirit,* entered the charts at No. 1 and became Britain's fastest-selling debut of all time. Her most successful single, "Bleeding Love," reached No. 1 in more than 30 countries and was the best-selling single worldwide in 2008 – the same year she was proclaimed "Top New Artist" by *Billboard* magazine.

She released her second album, *Echo* in 2009. Her third album, *Glassheart,* is scheduled for release in October 2012.

Simon Cowell was so wowed by Lewis that he phoned legendary music executive Clive Davis and told him, "You might have the next Whitney Houston on your hands." The two teamed up and signed Lewis to J Records/ Syco Music.

Olly Murs

As a teen, Olly Murs never thought music was the career path for him. The Essex native played semi-professional soccer and later worked as a recruiter for an employment agency.

That all charged in 2009, when he rose to fame as the runner-up in the sixth series of *The X Factor*.

In August 2010, Murs released his debut single, "Please Don't Let Me Go," which debuted at No. 1 on the UK singles charts, becoming Murs' second top-ranked single after releasing "You Are Not Alone" with the other Season 6 finalists.

The quirky, outspoken entertainer has since released two albums, both of which have sold well in the United Kingdom. In 2011, he returned to *The X Factor* to co-host the spin-off show *The Xtra Factor.*

He spent the first part of 2012 in the United States, supporting One Direction on their first North American headline tour.

Cher Lloyd

Cher Lloyd finished fourth in the seventh season of *The X Factor* but her post-show career has eclipsed those of her competitors.

The English rapper was signed by Simon Cowell to Syco Music. Her debut single, "Swagger Jagger," debuted at No. 1 on the UK singles chart and No. 2 on the Irish singles chart.

Lloyd's debut album, *Sticks + Stones,* peaked at No. 4 on the UK charts.

Now, Lloyd's making waves in the United States, doing a radio station tour and performing on television shows including *America's Got Talent*. In July 2012, the British singer's debut U.S. single, "Want U Back," shot to No. 7 on the iTunes chart.

Springsteen and Adele each down a notch. The previous highest entry for a UK group's first album was No. 6, when the Spice Girls entered the U.S. charts with *Spice* in 1997.

"We simply cannot believe that we are No. 1 in America," Harry told the *Coventry (England) Evening Telegraph* in March 2012. "It's beyond a dream come true for us. We want to thank each and every one of our fans in the U.S. who bought our album and we would also like to thank the American public for being so supportive of us."

In a statement released by the group's record label, Niall noted: "When we got put together as a group, we couldn't imagine ourselves coming to America, let alone releasing our album here, so for us to be sitting at the top of the U.S. album charts is unbelievable."

Within the first week of its release, One Direction sold more than 176,000 copies of its debut album, *Up All Night*. The CD shot straight to the top of the digital charts within minutes of its official release on March 13, 2012.

Music critic Mark Sutherland believes One Direction owes much of its enormous trans-Atlantic success to social media. Band members and management have fully embraced the use of Internet sites such as Facebook and Twitter as promotional tools.

One Direction is Minionized on Universal Orlando's new ride, Despicable Me Minion Mayham.

SIMON COWELL: *BRASH BUT SOMEHOW LOVEABLE*

Comedian Dane Cook once feted Simon Cowell with the musical tribute: "You have the honesty of Abe Lincoln and the charm of the guy who shot him."

That's Cowell. He's brutally honest, unapologetically brash, snarky and oftentimes just plain cruel.

Most Americans know Cowell as the multi-millionaire music mogul who verbally insulted contestants on *American Idol* and, more recently *X Factor USA*.

What most viewers don't realize is that Cowell isn't just a high-paid talent show judge. He's also one of the most successful people in the music industry – though he's hardly a musician himself. He doesn't sing or produce records; he can't even read music. So, what does he do?

"(I) guess what's going to be popular," he very succinctly told interviewer Anderson Cooper in 2007.

That ability to "guess" has served him well. He runs successful companies in Great Britain and the United States. In addition to hit television shows, he's a record executive for Sony BMG. He hangs out with A-list celebrities and owns lavish homes in London and Beverly Hills.

The son of a music industry executive and socialite/ballet dancer, Cowell got early exposure to the entertainment world. He dropped out of school at age 16 and worked odd jobs until his father got him a job with EMI Music Publishing. He started off doing errands and worked his way up the ladder until he got a job at EMI as a record producer. He eventually left that company to start his own small record labels. He later joined BMG where he helped launch the bands Five and Westlife.

Cowell made his first TV appearance in 2001 as a judge on UK talent show *Pop Idol,* which was later adapted in the United States as *American Idol.* Cowell helped make *American Idol* one of the most popular TV shows in the United States. In turn, the show helped make Cowell a celebrity in his own right.

He left *American Idol* in 2009 and has also been a celebrity judge on shows including *The X Factor* and *Britain's Got Talent*.

His *Syco* label signed the top two finishers of the first season of *Pop Idol,* Will Young and Gareth Gates, both of whom went on score No. 1 hits in the United Kingdom. More recently, his musical "creations" include the group Il Divo, a multinational operatic pop group that, to date, has sold more than 26 million albums worldwide.

Cowell, who has found himself on the covers of gossip magazines on more than one occasion, garnered headlines again in April 2012, when his new tell-all biography was released. Cowell reportedly cooperated on the book, written by former BBC journalist Tom Bower. Despite his involvement, *Sweet Revenge: The Intimate Life of Simon Cowell* paints a not-so-pretty picture of Cowell. Revelations in the book include:

- Staying healthy and young-looking are important to Cowell. He schedules regular colonic irrigations and gets Botox and weekly vitamin infusions.
- He is prone to "introspective monologues" that can go on for hours about his work, and his fear of failure.
- Cowell had an affair with former *X Factor* judge Danii Minogue.
- He gave his ex-fiancée Mezhgan Hussainy, a makeup artist on *American Idol*, a $5 million Beverly Hills house as a break-up gift.
- Cowell is obsessed with cleanliness. A former girlfriend reports he throws out spoons if they've been used to eat yogurt. He also likes to bathe and scrub twice a day, and can change his T-shirts up to four times daily.
- Black is the preferred color for toilet paper in the Cowell household.

Chapter 1:
BEAUTIFUL BEGINNINGS

"I think a few years ago they would have struggled to get the exposure," he said. "They've been quite clever with putting in a lot of groundwork with social media with the fans, so they had a lot of interest before they arrived in America."

That "interest" became obvious when, in March 2012, One Direction made its American television debut. A crowd of more than 10,000 screaming fans showed up for the group's *Today* show taping at Rockefeller Center, prompting NBC to hire dozens of additional security guards.

"The *Today* show for me was the most amazing thing," Liam told *The Washington Post*. "There wasn't enough room for everybody to come up. They couldn't even see us. They were just hanging around to get a glimpse of what's going on."

Young fans already knew these guys were the real deal and their reaction made the rest of American sit up and take notice.

The guys themselves were gob-smacked by their success in the United States.

During an interview with Vevo Life, Louis admitted their success – at least its magnitude – was rather unexpected.

"It's really surprising for us that we'd get like a good reception here in America because obviously we came off a UK TV show, we did the first music video here and all of a sudden, people started recognizing us."

One Direction visits Six Flags Magic Mountain in Valencia, California.

M

THE INFLUX OF TV TALENT SHOWS

The guys from One Direction can thank *The X Factor* for putting them on the Fame Train, but they're hardly the first artists to have benefited from a reality television competition. In fact, TV talent shows have been around since the 1940s, when folks tuned in to watch the *Original Amateur Hour* or *Arthur Godfrey's Talent Scouts.*

Star Search was among the United States' longest-running TV talent shows. It was produced from 1983-95 and hosted by Ed McMahon (a re-launch was produced from 2003-2004). This particular competition featured categories for vocalists, comedians, dancers and spokesmodels. Some of the most notable musical contestants on the original *Star Search* include Alanis Morissette (1988), Beyonce (1993), Britney Spears (1994), Christina Aguilera (1994) and Justin Timberlake (1993).

Dozens of other shows, including *America's Got Talent, American Idol, The Voice, I Wanna Be A Soap Star, So You Think You Can Dance, Making the Band, Nashville Star* and *The X Factor*, have catapulted amateur artists to fame.

American Idol, a reality singing competition based on the UK show *Pop Idol,* began airing on June 11, 2002. Kelly Clarkson, Carrie Underwood, Jordin Sparks, David Cook, Clay Aiken, Katharine McPhee and Kellie Pickler are among *Idol* contestants who have found fame, in large part due to their exposure on the show.

Of course, these shows are not simply an American phenomenon. In fact, the

Host Ed McMahon and comedian Jerry Lewis chat on the set of *Star Search* on November 3, 1983, in Los Angeles, California.

H.P. Baxxter, Sarah Conner, Sandra Nasic, and Moses Pelahm attend the *X Factor* press conference at Lofthaus on July 3, 2012, in Dusseldorf, Germany.

genre has included as many as 600 different shows in 104 nations.

The X Factor is Europe's biggest television talent competition – having peaked with 19.7 million UK viewers (a 63.2 percent audience share).

Sir David Jason says he appreciates the popularity of TV talent competitions but at the same time calls them "voyeuristic" and "cruel." The veteran British actor says he believes the shows tend to bring out the mean-spiritedness of audiences.

"Sometimes bits of television talent shows can be quite cruel and that's sort of the object of the exercise," he told *The (London) Telegraph*. "They wouldn't have put on a show to show all the best every night all the time, it would be dull wouldn't it? So, they have to show you some of the less talented people in order to make us lot go, 'Ooh look at that, he's no good is he? He can't do nothing.'"

Toby Young, British writer and self-proclaimed "mean" judge on *Top Chef* says the cold hard truth is that TV audiences like watching other people suffer. A flawless jitterbug is nice, but fans don't get really excited until a contestant falls on a dancing show or has a judge tell him he's "pitchy" on a singing show.

"It was true of the Romans and it's true of us. Reality TV is the 21st century equivalent of the gladiatorial arena," he said.

Chapter 1:
BEAUTIFUL BEGINNINGS

Louis, Harry, Liam, Zayn, and Niall perform live at Gibson Amphitheatre on June 16, 2012, in Universal City, California.

And that "good reception" just keeps coming. According to the music analysts at Nielsen, *Up All Night* was the third-best-selling U.S. album of the first half of 2012 with 899,000 copies sold. One Direction's management company, Modest! Management, reports that as of June 2012, the album had sold over 2.7 million copies worldwide.

But signs of the guys' popularity don't start and end with record sales. Tickets for the group's May/June 2012 tour sold out in minutes, and their December 3, 2012, show at Madison Square Garden sold out in less than 10 minutes. By mid-July 2012, the band's group and individual Twitter accounts had a combined 29.6 million followers. They'd also racked up more than 8.1 million "likes" on their official Facebook page and 460 million views of their YouTube videos.

When you look back on all that success it's hard to wonder "What If?" and far better to shout out, "Thank goodness!"

SIMON'S TOUCH NOT ALWAYS GOLDEN

As far-reaching as Simon Cowell's entertainment industry super powers seem to be, he's had his share of missteps. A few of his acts that have not achieved mega-fame include:

Girl Thing was a British girl band made up of members Jodi Albert, Anika Bostelaar, Linzi Martin, Michelle Barber and Nikki Stuart. The group's biggest hit, "Last One Standing," peaked at No. 8 on the UK Singles Chart in 2000. When Girl Thing's second single, "Girls on Top," failed to break the Top 20, their album release was cancelled in Great Britain. Barber recalled the disappointment in a Nov. 2010 interview with the (London) *Daily Mail*: "When it all went wrong, Simon just vanished in a puff of smoke."

5ive (or Five) was Cowell's first try at a boy band. The group was created after several rounds of auditions in London in 1997. The band was signed by Cowell for a six-album deal. Five enjoyed some success and even managed to have a hit in America. Group members, however, couldn't get along, so decided to split up in 2001. The group – minus one member – briefly reformed in 2006 under new management but soon disbanded again.

Matt Cardle, Simon Cowell's first act to sign a joint deal between his own Syco Music and Columbia, was dumped by his record company in July 2012. Cardle, who won the 2010 edition of *The X Factor,* had publicly and repeatedly badmouthed both Cowell and *The X Factor.*

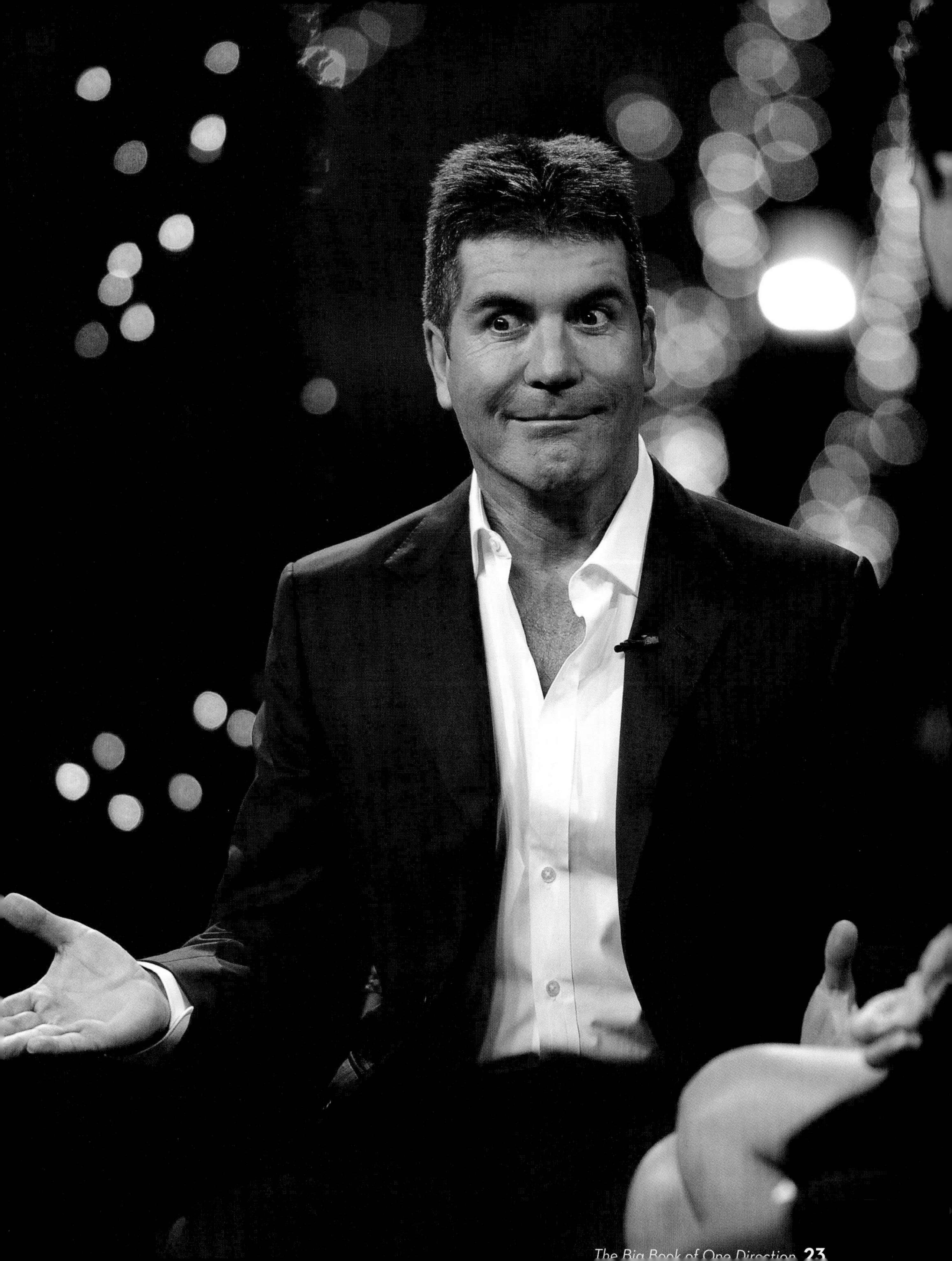

Chapter 2:
WORLDWIDE SUCCESS

Chapter 2:
WORLDWIDE SUCCESS

When the bigwigs at NBC's *Today* show booked newcomers One Direction to appear on the morning show March 12, 2012, they had no idea what they were in for. Network executives are, after all, not in the band's key demographic. How were they to know that 10,000 adoring, screaming fans would flock to New York City's Rockefeller Plaza that day for the band's American television debut?

The crowd was among the largest *Today* has ever seen for its free concert series - only Justin Bieber, Lady Gaga and Chris Brown have drawn that kind of turnout to date.

Melissa Lonner, senior entertainment producer for *Today*, expressed a combination of awe and disbelief when she was interviewed by *Billboard* magazine shortly after the event.

"Keep in mind, Justin and Chris have had hits in the U.S. and are known in the U.S.," she said. "One Direction is relatively unknown with no hits yet. They basically exploded, and all the adults are saying, 'Who are these people, and how do they know about it?'"

The enormous crowd required additional security and the ensuing pandemonium made folks sit up and take notice. Radio stations played 1D's songs with more frequency. They were contacted for media interviews. Their legion of followers on social network platforms was growing daily. American fans were anxious to hear and see the United Kingdom's hottest new export.

It wasn't long before One Direction's breakout single, "What Makes You Beautiful," became the highest-charting debut for a U.K. artist on the Billboard Hot 100 since Jimmy Ray's 1998 hit "Are You Jimmy Ray?"

Just 10 days after its *Today* appearance, One Direction became the first U.K. group ever to debut at No. 1 on the U.S. Billboard 200 album chart. The band sold 176,000 copies of its debut album, *Up All Night*, within the first week of its release.

On July 27, 2012, Billboard announced that One Direction's *Up All Night* album crossed the 1 million sales mark, becoming only the second set to hit a million for the year - Adele's *21* sold 3.8 million copies in 2012.

The UK band's popularity quickly escalated to levels of such enormity that many began to note its similarity to Beatlemania that hit New York back in 1964.

GOTTA BE QUICK

If you waited 11 seconds, you were too late. Ticketmaster sold out One Direction's first headline tour of United Kingdom and Ireland in a record 10.6 seconds when they went on sale Oct. 1, 2011.

Harry on the red carpet for the premiere of the Nickelodeon TV movie *Big Time Movie* in New York on Thursday, March 8, 2012. (AP Photo/Charles Sykes)

Chapter 2:
WORLDWIDE SUCCESS

Louis, Niall, Harry, Liam, and Zayn perform live at Trusts Stadium on April 21, 2012, in Auckland, New Zealand.

Sonny Takhar, Syco's musical director, attributes the speed at which everything is happening to the power of social media.

"Sometimes you feel the song's the star, but it's not like that here – it's the act," he told *The (UK) Guardian*. "It's a real moment. Social media has become the new radio; it's never broken an act globally like this before."

And so, the Tweets and Facebook posts continue to feed the fervor.

The band's in-store signings and appearances have shut down malls across the United States. Fans – mostly young females – have camped outside their hotels and sneaked backstage in hopes of catching a glimpse of the lads.

One Direction headlined its first concert tour beginning in December 2011. The tour was announced in September 2011 with the first shows being in Great Britain and Ireland. After just a month – and due to considerable international demand – the tour was expanded with legs in Australia and North America.

Louis performs live on stage at Hinsense Arena on April 16, 2012, in Melbourne, Australia.

Zayn performs live on stage at Horden Pavilion on April 13, 2012, in Sydney, Australia.

AN OPENING ACT - AT AGE 13?!?

Camryn Magness just became an official teenager on July 14, 2012. She became an official pop star years earlier.

Camryn (in the music business, she's known only by her first name) was 10 years old when she recorded her first single, "Wait and See," with Frank Schooflar of the band Blessed By A Broken Heart and longtime family friend Lennon Murphy.

Her first big break came in 2011, when director John Schultz selected "Wait and See" as the title track for his film adaptation of the children's book *Judy Moody and the Not Bummer Summer*. The song enjoyed moderate success, peaking at No. 38 on the *Billboard* charts. Its music video was shot on the former set of TV's *Hannah Montana* and featured *Family Matters* star Jaleel White.

Camryn's second single, "Set The Night On Fire," was also written by Camryn, Frank Schooflar and Lennon Murphy. It debuted on Top 40 radio in the United States in May 2012.

As if having a couple of songs being played on the radio wasn't enough, in April 2011 it was announced that Camryn had joined Cody Simpson and Greyson Chance on their Waiting 4U Tour. During fall 2011, Camryn launched a Back 2 School Tour, performing at nearly 100 schools and for over 80,000 students.

Then, in spring and summer 2012, Camryn hit the road with 1D on their Up All Night Tour of the United States.

"The boys are awesome," Camryn told *SugarScape* in June 2012. "They are very random, spontaneous and funny. Harry loves to start random dance parties any time he hears music. Every time he'd walk past my dressing room I'd catch him dancing to the music we were playing."

Camryn, who is homeschooled, describes herself as self-motivated. The teen comes from a show-biz family; her parents are movie producers Gary Magness and Sarah Siegel-Magness (*Precious*).

"When I was eight, I decided that this is what I wanted to do," Camryn told the *(Minneapolis) Star-Tribune* in April 2011.

Chapter 2:
WORLDWIDE SUCCESS

TicketNews reported that tickets to all of 1D's 2012 dates sold out within hours of going on sale and the band's special performance at Madison Square Garden on December 3 sold out in less than 10 minutes. Almost immediately, the price of tickets to these shows doubled and tripled in price on the secondary market. A front row ticket to the group's June 23, 2012, show in Dallas, for example, was going for more than $1,600.

In an effort to dry the tears of the fans who couldn't get tickets for the 2012 tour, One Direction announced on April 12, 2012, that the band would be headlining a 2013 World Tour.

The World Tour kicks off Feb. 22 with four shows at London's O2 Arena and returns to the states in June 2013.

PICKIN' AND GRINNIN'

Swedish born Rami Yacoub and Carl Falk penned the hit "What Makes You Beautiful" for One Direction, as well as follow-up single "One Thing," alongside collaborator Savan Kotecha. What's the trick to writing for 1D?

"The important thing is that fans should be able to play (the songs) on an acoustic guitar and post it to YouTube," Falk told *Variety* magazine.

The strategy seems to be working. The amateur covers of "What Makes You Beautiful" on YouTube now number in the thousands.

DOCUMENTARY DELIGHT

One Direction: A Year in the Making, a documentary telling the story of 1D's rise to fame, made its TV debut on July 14, 2012. The behind-the-scenes film follows the guys from their auditions for *The X Factor* and recording their album, to traveling on their first tour and becoming worldwide sensations.

One Direction performs at the Bank Atlantic Center in Sunrise, Florida, on Sunday, July 1, 2012. (Robert Duyos/Sun Sentinel/MCT via Getty Images).

Harry performs live on stage during the evening performance at Hordern Pavilion on April 13, 2012, in Sydney, Australia. (Photo by Don Arnold/WireImage).

Chapter 2:
WORLDWIDE SUCCESS

Alas, many of those shows sold out as quickly as tickets became available – oftentimes 12 to 16 months ahead of the actual show.

Noting that the band will have performed at least 171 live shows by the time they end their tour in New Zealand in October 2013, Andy Green, associate editor of *Rolling Stone*, said: "One Direction could eclipse the big-tour megabucks earned by rock giants U2 and The Rolling Stones.

"I've never known a band to announce a second summer tour before a first summer tour is over," he added. "It's insane – they're working them like dogs and printing money right now."

For their part, the guys say they're up for the "hard work" that staying in the game long-term entails. They know fans can be fickle and fame can be fleeting – rest now and this tour could be their last.

"The music industry moves so fast you have to be on your toes," Niall told *We Love Pop* magazine. "Lady Gaga is at the peak of her career, but it could all go from under her. She's stopping that by bringing out song after song and keeping people interested. We're lucky because we've got a good fan base, but if they don't like our music, how long is that going to last?"

In hopes of striking while the fire is hot, the group has been busy recording a second album in London – and doing media interviews and making TV

1D GLEEKS?

Directioners and Gleeks rejoiced – together – when Fox TV's *Glee* cast performed a cover of One Direction's "What Makes You Beautiful." The performance came during the show's May 8, 2012 episode, called "Prom-asaurus."

Zayn, Harry, Niall, Liam, and Louis pose at BBC Radio One on August 10, 2011, in London, England.

Chapter 2:
WORLDWIDE SUCCESS

THE CRITICS HAVE SPOKEN ...

Tweens, teens and their parents have snatched up tickets to One Direction's earliest shows. Their fans clearly adore them, but what do music critics around the world have to say? Here are snippets from reviews of some of their earliest arena shows:

"Often it was (Zayn Malik) or Mr. Styles carrying the vocals, with Mr. Payne not far behind. Mr. Horan, partial to drop-crotch trousers, was easily distractible, and Mr. Tomlinson was the chattiest."

- Jon Caramanica in *The New York Times*, May 27, 2012

"Unlike most of their antecedents, 1D (as they're known to fans) don't fall back on choreography or pre-recorded vocal sweetening - the members don't have much in the way of dance moves, and occasionally wobble as they warble. That lends a sense of vulnerability to the proceedings and also imparts a degree of authenticity - one that belies the laboratory genesis of the group, which was assembled for the British

edition of *X Factor*."
- David Sprague in *Variety*, May 27, 2012.

"Overall, One Direction owned the crowd. They worked it. They spoke to their fans, as opposed to speaking above them. They put themselves on the same level and make themselves easy to relate to, when you're a 14-year-old, of course."
- Amy Sciarretto in *ArtistDirect*, May 29, 2012

"Watching the boys of One Direction live is like watching an Abercrombie & Fitch catalogue come to life. The show is divided into seasons, which beg for outfit changes, while the crowd screams at video interludes of the boys surfing and snowboarding. It's easy to get lost in the inherent appeal of their perfectly coiffed dos and almost-too-put-together preppy style but somewhere in the midst of all the love-struck squeals of teenage girls are guys who can actually sing and, to a certain extent, entertain."
- Melody Lau in the *(Canada) National Post*, June 1, 2012

"The crowd ate it up. Every movement, every sigh, every note and every joke were greeted with ear-splitting screams. Plus, the cellphones were in full force. The blond girl standing next to me was trembling so much that she had to steady her phone with the 1D light tube in her other hand."
- Mario Tarradell in *The Dallas Morning News*, June 24, 2012

"That the cumulative EEEEEEEE! was akin to a panicked parakeet lodged in your ear is not the point. A very, very sold-out 1-800-Ask-Gary Amphitheatre was absolutely packed with pure joy. If you were of the older, chaperonial persuasion, you might have left with a headache or an earache or a desire to flee to Mexico. But you also might have left with a lump in your throat."
- Sean Daly in *Tampa Bay (Fla.) Times*, June 30, 2012

"Their smooth vocals sounded surprisingly strong and steady, traits that don't come easy for new artists stepping out on their first international tour. With a backing band and a massive video screen supporting the group, they were able to stride and pose around the stage with ease. There was no choreography or set routine here; slight hand motions and smiles were all they needed to win these girls' hearts."
- Brenna Rushing in *(Dallas-Fort Worth) Pegasus News*, June 29, 2012

Chapter 2:
WORLDWIDE SUCCESS

Left to right: Louis, Niall, Harry, Liam, and Zayn perform live at Gibson Amphitheatre on June 16, 2012, in Universal City, California.

appearances and signing copies of their book and promoting their behind-the-scenes documentary. These guys are leading busy, busy lives that are further complicated by the fact that they can't go anywhere without security. They can't simply decide to drop in at a skate park or go shopping or head to the movies without causing a mob scene. It's a level of success and stardom that has taken even the lads by surprise.

"We never expected any of this at all. We thought that we would do a little bit in the UK after the end of the show," Liam told STV (Sweden TV) in July 2012. "Now it has gone all over the world and more things have happened to us than we would ever have imagined. We owe it all to our fans... they are incredible and they have got us this far."

WRITE STUFF

British songster Ed Sheeran ("Moments") and *American Idol* winner Kelly Clarkson ("Tell Me A Lie") both wrote tracks for *Up All Night*.

Yes, yes, the fans made it all happen. But Simon Cowell, who signed 1D to his Syco Records imprint after the group's 2010 appearance on the U.K. version of *The X Factor*, says pop star

TOP DEBUT ALBUMS IN U.S. HISTORY

One Direction made history when it became the first U.K. group ever to debut at No. 1 on the Billboard 200 album chart. That puts the guys in some pretty elite company.

The following are the biggest selling debut albums in United States history. The sales totals come from the Recording Industry Association of America (RIAA):

No.	Artist	Album	Year	Sales Total
1.	Guns N' Roses	*Appetite For Destruction*	1987	18 million
2.	Boston	*Boston*	1976	17 million
3.	Alanis Morissette	*Jagged Little Pill*	1995	16 million
4.	Hootie and the Blowfish	*Cracked Rear View*	1994	16 million
5.	Backstreet Boys	*Backstreet Boys*	1997	14 million
6.	Britney Spears	*Baby One More Time*	1999	14 million
7.	Pearl Jam	*Ten*	1991	13 million
8.	Whitney Houston	*Whitney Houston*	1985	13 million
9.	Matchbox 20	*Yourself or Someone Like You*	1996	12 million
10.	Jewel	*Pieces of You*	1995	12 million
11.	Linkin Park	*Hybrid Theory*	2000	10 million
12.	George Michael	*Faith*	1987	10 million
13.	Garth Brooks	*Garth Brooks*	1989	10 million
14.	Norah Jones	*Come Away With Me*	2002	10 million
15.	Van Halen	*Van Halen*	1978	10 million
16.	N'Sync	*N'Sync*	1998	10 million
17.	Nelly	*Country Grammer*	2000	9 million
18.	Mariah Carey	*Mariah Carey*	1990	9 million
19.	Billy Ray Cyrus	*Some Gave All*	1992	9 million
20.	Beastie Boys	*License to Ill*	1986	9 million

Chapter 2:
WORLDWIDE SUCCESS

Justin Bieber and his manager, Scooter Braun, also deserve some credit for 1D's success. After all, it was Bieber who made young adult stars cool again.

"I've done this long enough that everything in music and entertainment is cyclical," Cowell told *Billboard* in March 2012. "(Even if) you go back to the Motown days, every time, it always comes back to 12 o'clock. It felt like that time again."

The guys are grateful for everything Cowell has done for them, but they're quick to point out that they are, indeed, real artists – not puppets being told every move they should make. They even got writing credits for a couple tracks on *Up All Night*.

"Songwriting's a very precious thing, you know," Zayn told *The Irish Times* in January 2012. "When you write your own music you can be quite precious about it, and it can be quite hard to express it to people. But we always felt comfortable. And we had each other to show our ideas to."

Left to right: Louis, Liam, Harry, Zayn, and Niall travel in a luxury helicopter to Glasgow, Manchester, and London on September 11, 2011. The tour was taken to launch their first single, "What Makes You Beautiful."

ONE DIRECTION VS. BEATLES – AT A GLANCE

Fans, music critics and even One Direction vocalist Harry Styles have pointed out that there are similarities between One Direction and the Beatles. After all, both British boy bands managed great success in the states, sending fans into absolute delirium. But, what are the similarities – or differences – beyond that? We offer this quick look at the two monstrously popular groups:

	One Direction	**The Beatles**
The guys	Harry, Liam, Louis, Niall and Zayn	George, John, Paul and Ringo
Years active	2010-present	1960-1970
Roadblocks along the way	Auditioned as individuals for TV's *The X Factor* but didn't make the cut. Judge Nicole Scherzinger suggested they compete as a group and the guys agreed.	Dick Rowe of Decca Records took a pass on the group at their 1962 audition, saying that "guitar groups were on their way out." Decca's rejection is now considered one of the biggest mistakes in music history. The group went on to sign with EMI subsidiary Parlophone.
First U.S. TV appearance	*The Today Show,* March 2012	*The Ed Sullivan Show,* January 1964
First U.S. single	"What Makes You Beautiful," 2012	"I Want to Hold Your Hand," 1963
Biggest flirt	Harry Styles	Paul McCartney
Trademark hair style	A little messy, looks windswept even when there's no wind	Mop tops in the early years then, in the late 1960s, longer locks and facial hair
Fashion statement	School-boy prep, often color-coordinated among the band-mates.	During the Beatles' first U.S. tour, John Lennon wore a black fisher-man's cap which became popularly known as a "John Lennon Hat." His other signature piece? Round, thin-rimmed glasses, still referred to as "John Lennon glasses."

ONE DIRECTION VS BEATLES – AT A GLANCE

	One Direction	The Beatles
Brit Quotient?	80 percent (Niall Horan is from Ireland.)	100 percent (All from Liverpool)
Fans	Directioners	Beatlemaniacs
Strummers and drummers?	Not so much. Niall strums a bit and you'll see some air drumming, but that's it for these guys.	Yes. Between the four, they played the guitar, bass, harmonica, keyboards, sitar and drums.
Girl troubles	Harry Styles' preference for dating "cougars," most notably British TV personality Caroline Flack who is 15 years his senior, sparked a media frenzy.	Yoko Ono's romance with John Lennon was hardly the only factor straining the relationships between the members of the Beatles, but she got the majority of the blame when the group broke up. She also took considerable criticism for the influence she held over Lennon, both in his personal life and his music.
Controversy	There's the matter of a $1 million lawsuit and countersuit over the use of the band's name. Plus, the group has garnered plenty of negative press over Harry Style's fondness for older – sometimes married – women, and a July 2012 incident in which Niall Horan was caught on video swearing at fans.	There were a number of controversies along the way but none bigger than when John Lennon told a reporter: "We're more popular than Jesus now." The quote ran in a British newspaper in March 1966 with little reaction. However, outrage ensued when the statement was reprinted in the American teen magazine *Datebook* six months later. Fans burned albums, mounted protests and convinced radio stations to ban Beatles music.

Niall performs at the Bank Atlantic Center in Sunrise, Florida, on July 1, 2012.

Fans wait in anticipation for the teen pop group at the Bank Atlantic Center in Sunrise, Florida, on July 1, 2012.

Chapter 3:

CHEEKY NIALL

Chapter 3:
CHEEKY NIALL

The Horan family photo album includes a candid picture of four-year-old Niall, dressed in a sweater and khakis, singing into a toy microphone while strumming a plastic guitar. It's a living room concert that, from the looks of other photos in the album, was a common occurrence during his childhood.

"He really is doing what he wanted to do since he was born," Niall's father, Bobby Horan, told *The (London) Sun* in April 2012. "All the photos of him as a child prove it."

Who would have guessed that the rosy-cheeked boy in that album would become one-fifth of a band that's gone on to set sales records on both sides of the Atlantic?

Niall was born in Mullingar in County Westmeath, located in the north-central part of Ireland. His parents, Bobby and Maura, divorced when he was just five years old.

At first, Niall and his brother, Greg, who is six years older, went to live with their mother. After a year, though, the boys returned to live with their father.

"They came home one night and that was it, they told me they'd decided to stay," Bobby told *The (London) Daily Mirror*. "I was very lonely for that year without them so, of course, I was really happy to have them back. I had a family around me again."

Niall's upbringing was fairly typical. His father worked – and still does – as a butcher at a Mullingar supermarket. His mother, who worked at Mullingar Pewter and has since remarried, stayed close to her sons thanks to frequent visits and calls.

"They lived with me but their mother was very involved and we made decisions together," Bobby said. "Niall always had two birthday parties ... one here and one at his mum's and whenever she wanted to see them she would come over. We still get on very well."

Because he spent much of his childhood with a single father, Niall was forced to take on household chores.

"He had to look after himself a lot because I was working, so from the age of seven he had to do his own washing, his own ironing

BIRD'S THE WORD

Niall is a ornithophobic.

The truth is, he's not so frightened by hummingbirds or bluebirds. It's pigeons that have him scared silly.

Niall admits his fear stems from an incident when a particularly foul fowl flew through his bathroom window.

"I can't stand them after one once flew in through my bathroom window and went for me while I was having a wee. That was enough," he told *The (London) Sun*. "I get really nervous if pigeons are flying around before shows. I think pigeons target me."

Niall performs on stage at Nickelodeon's 25th Annual Kids' Choice Awards at Galen Center on March 31, 2012, in Los Angeles, California.

and often his own cooking," Bobby recalled. "When he was at school I tried to get home for 4.30 p.m., but I started early mornings, so Niall had to get himself up and walk the mile-and-a-half to school."

His parents say that even as a young boy, Niall had a sense of fashion and flair. "He always dressed himself well and had a nice style about him. He never left the house without making sure he looked good," Bobby said.

Niall's cousin, Robert Horan, told the *(London) Daily Mail* in 2010 that he'd long envisioned Niall would end up in the entertainment industry.

"Even when he was a young child, I said to myself, 'That lad is going to end up on the stage' – though I always thought he'd end up being a comedian," said Robert. "Niall was always really outgoing and quick-witted, always yapping away."

Young Niall began his theatrical "career" in a production of *Oliver!* at St. Kenny National School, where he was often selected to sing solos with the school choir.

Deputy Principal Ann Caulfield recalled Niall's primary school days with affection.

"He is remembered for his manners and his personality as much as his singing," she told *Independent News & Media* in December 2010.

"He was a little saintly child in the classroom and every other teacher would say the same – a very, very good boy."

ARE YOU THE NIALL HORAN

Teen pop star or 31-year-old insurance worker – which are you following on Twitter? They are, after all, both named Niall Horan.

The older, non-singing, brunette Horan lives in Tipperary, Ireland, and – thanks to his famous moniker – he's amassed more than 5,000 followers.

"My Twitter followers rocketed after One Direction became famous in America this year," "Insurance" Niall told *The (London) Mirror* in July 2012. "But I had the name – my real one – on Twitter before Niall the singer so I am not going to change it because he's famous."

He's done his best to warn that he's not the man fans are looking for, but many have ignored his advice. Additionally, Tipperary Niall reveals he's gotten phone calls from fans who've tracked down his mobile number in the mistaken belief he's the singer.

Ah, such is the price of almost fame.

As a secondary school student, Niall became a more frequent performer. Teacher Georgina Ainscough, who organized the talent shows there, described Niall as genuine and hardworking.

"He's a natural-born performer,"

ABOUT NIALL

Full name:	Niall James Horan
Hometown:	Mullinger, Westmeath, Ireland
Birthdate:	September 13, 1993
Astrological sign:	Virgo
***The X Factor* audition song:**	"So Sick of Love Songs"
Favorite American food:	Everything that's edible
Favorite flicks:	*Grease*
Favorite Pokemon:	Roggenrola
Celebrity crush:	Actress/singer Miranda Cosgrove
If there was a One Direction movie, actor who might portray him:	*Harry Potter* actor Tom Felton
On Twitter:	@NiallOfficial
Twitter followers:	5.20 million as of July 2012

Chapter 3:
CHEEKY NIALL

Ainscough told the *(London) Daily Mail*. "He is so motivated and bubbly and he's always smiling."

When Niall decided to pack his bags and try his luck at *The X Factor* auditions, it was with the full support of his family, friends and teachers. In fact, his grandmother and mother escorted him to Dublin, where he tried out for the TV talent show.

The blond teenager sailed through the auditions and call-backs, only to be eliminated at boot camp. Then, quite famously, the judges stepped in and gave Niall and four other handpicked hopefuls a second chance, if they were willing to compete as a group.

As the competition continued, so did the support, with Niall's friends and family attending performances whenever possible.

His grandmother, Margaret Nolan, was thrilled to be in the crowd when Niall and the guys hit the stage to sing Coldplay's "Viva La Vida" for *The X Factor*'s first live show.

"'It was overwhelming being there, seeing how massive it all is, but it was

POTTY MOUTH

Niall made headlines around the world when video appeared of him referring to some female fans using a derogatory – and unprintable – term.

On July 6, 2012, he took to Twitter to apologize: "Really sorry if I caused any offense. It was just banter with fans who I think of more as mates. But I understand that it's not a word I should be using at all."

Apology accepted, Niall. Just don't do it again.

Niall attends the *Men In Black 3* New York premiere at Ziegfeld Theatre on May 23, 2012.

Niall performs at the Beacon Theatre on May 26, 2012, in New York City.

NIALL'S HOMETOWN

Westmeath is the 20th largest of Ireland's 32 counties; its government offices are located in Niall Horan's hometown: Mullingar.

The town, population 17,300, has a significant agricultural history. More recently, the town's economy has become reliant on its strong industrial and technical base. One of Mullingar's major exports is pewter ware produced by the firm of Mullingar Pewter. With lakes Owel, Ennell and Derravaragh nearby, Mullingar's locale is particularly scenic. The water attracts fishermen from miles around; the area is also well suited to outdoor activities including hiking, horseback riding and golf.

There are shopping centers both downtown and on the outskirts of town. The city is also home to libraries, gymnasiums, pubs, cafes, an arts center and a railway station.

Tourist attractions include a greyhound track, Belvedere House Gardens & Park, and St. Munna's, which was originally built as a parish church around the middle of the 15th century.

Niall has long been supported by his fellow residents. In fact, when he appeared on *The X Factor* in 2010, this notice appeared in the Mullingar Parish church bulletin: *We encourage all our parishioners to support Niall Horan and One Direction in this year's X Factor. Niall began his singing life as a pupil at St. Kenny's School and has often sung in the Cathedral as a student in Coláiste Mhuire.*

Other famous Mullingar residents include:

- Singer **Joe Dolan** who was an energetic and charismatic Irish entertainer and singer of easy-listening songs.
- Author **J.P. Donleavy** who won critical acclaim for his first novel, *The Ginger Man.*
- Author, theatrical producer and TV presenter **Josephine Hart** who wrote the novel *Damage,* which was the basis for the 1992 film of the same name.
- Actress **Tina Kellegher** who is best known for her role as Niamh Quigley in BBC television series *Ballykissangel.*
- Boxer **John Joe Nevin**, an Irish traveler who won the Irish National Boxing Title and qualified for the 2008 and 2012 Summer Olympics.
- **Michael O'Leary** who is the Chief Executive Officer of the Irish airline Ryanair; he is also one of Ireland's wealthiest businessmen.

great and Niall loves that. We sat with all the other One Direction families, they were all lovely," Margaret told *The Daily Mail* in 2010. "It was absolutely brilliant, the most exciting thing I've ever done. I've been to London in my time, but never at anything like this. With everyone cheering for my grandson up on the stage, I was the proudest granny in Ireland."

In the two years since One Direction skyrocketed to fame thanks to *The X Factor*, Niall's life has changed dramatically. Gone are the days of anonymously hanging out with his buddies while cheering on the Derby County football team. There's no more hanging out in the mall food court. No more quietly catching some rays on the beach.

These days, hundreds – if not thousands – of fans seem to show up wherever he goes. Mobs materialize outside hotel rooms and arena entrances. Scores of shrieking, crying, arm-waving teens have gone so far as to chase the band's bus and then rock it side to side.

"There are hordes of young girls around

Niall smiles while at the Beacon Theatre on May 26, 2012, in New York City.

Niall performs at The Brisbane Convention and Exhibition Centre on April 18, 2012, in Australia.

IRISH TO THE CORE

Niall is clearly proud of his Irish heritage. Directioners who dream of cuddling up with this crooner would be wise to study up on some Irish basics. For starters:
His flag. The national flag of Ireland is frequently referred to as the Irish tricolor. It has vertical bands of green, white and orange.
His capital. Dublin is Ireland's capital – as well as its largest city.
His anthem: The Irish national anthem is called "The Soldier's Song." Its chorus begins: "Soldiers are we whose lives are pledged to Ireland."
His national motto. Fé Mhóid Bheith Saor (Sworn to be free).
His national sport. Ireland's official national sport is hurling. It's an ancient Gaelic game in which players use wooden sticks called hurleys to hit a small ball called a sliotar between the opponent's goalposts. Hurling's sometimes referred to as "a cross between lacrosse and field hockey."
His slang. Irish jargon can be a bit confusing to non-natives. You may want to try out some more common slang terms, should you ever get the chance to chat with Niall:

Aye	-	Yes *(Aye, I'll go out with you!)*
Banjaxed	-	Broken *(My heart would be banjaxed if you quit the band.)*
Buck	-	A boy or man *(I didn't see many bucks at the concert.)*
Fierce	-	Very *(That was a fierce good song.)*
Gaff	-	House *(Want to come to my gaff for dinner?)*
Gowl	-	Annoying, stupid person *(Only a gowl wouldn't love One Direction.)*
Jammy	-	Lucky person *(Who was the jammy who got to go on stage?)*
Tool	-	Idiot *(The tool next to me talked throughout the entire show.)*
Wireless	-	The radio. *(Shhh! "Up All Night" is playing on the wireless.)*
Yank	-	American on holiday in Ireland. *(Would you and the guys like to show a yank the sights?)*

Niall attends a CD signing at Walmart on March 17, 2012, in Somerdale, New Jersey.

him, and not much room to breathe anywhere. He says it can be frightening," Bobby Horan told *The Mirror*. "Coming out of airports and girls crowding around their cars, he's started to get really claustrophobic."

While gaggles of girls make him nervous, Niall does love the ladies. He is the only member of One Direction who has not had a serious girlfriend since the group became uber-famous, but he's happy to use his finely tuned flirting skills to woo female celebrities.

Hundreds of articles and blog posts have tracked his crush-maybe-romance-no-just-friends relationship with songstress Demi Lovato. Similar media coverage has been devoted to Niall's charming interactions with singer/actress Selena Gomez (reportedly angering Gomez's boyfriend Justin Bieber) and reported liaisons with television presenter Amanda Byram and Harry Styles' ex-girlfriend, Alahna Aldridge.

Niall understands that being in the media spotlight is part of the deal when you are – well, in the spotlight. He may have occasional frustrations with the lack of privacy but, overall, he's thrilled to be able to perform on a world stage.

His friends and family are delighted that Niall has stayed so grounded, yet they fear his trusting nature makes him susceptible to those who only want his money.

"We worry that he could be ruined by gold diggers," a close pal told *The Mirror* in July 2012. "But Niall has a good head on his shoulders and he has good people behind him."

Niall's brother, Greg, echoed those concerns: "You do worry about things because he's my wee brother and you don't want to see him get used. You do wonder about people's intentions so you have to be careful.

"Some pictures and some stories worry

GIVE THAT GUY A GOLD MEDAL

In the same way fans go crazy for 1D, band member Niall went wild for the Olympic Games, often tweeting his thoughts about the festivities:

- "Don't know if it's just me, but the excitement in London is unbelievable! It's gonna be a great games."
- "Do they have an egg and spoon race in the Olympics? I wanna try. Always did well at sports day."
- "All the Irish athletes competing at #London2012, good luck to all of you! As usual your country is standing right behind you!"
- "Shout to fellow Mullingar man @johnJoeNevin who is goin strong at the Olympics. The whole country is behind ya bro including myself, good luck."

Niall makes a surprise visit to Westfield London Shopping Centre on August 2, 2012.

Chapter 3:
CHEEKY NIALL

Niall and One Direction attend a CD signing at J&R Music World in New York, on Monday, March 12, 2012. (AP Photo/Charles Sykes)

Dad. It's only natural to worry, but Niall's his own man and has been since for ages. He's very mature and independent so that has stood to him. He's on such a high now, he's living the dream so we don't want that to end. I want Niall's career to go on forever."

And, for those times when the hysterical fans and media scrutiny are too much to handle, Niall can rest easy knowing he can always go back to Mullingar. His father happily maintains his son's old bedroom – for those rare days off, when the superstar wants to get away from it all.

"I converted the garage for him because his guitar playing was making such a noise and we're so close to the house next door," says Bobby. "When he comes home he just wants to be Niall and leave Niall from One

Niall performs at the St. James Theatre in Wellington, New Zealand, on April 22, 2012.

Direction behind.

"I know it's pretty hard for him to get away but here in town, everyone's very proud of him but no one bothers him. He's through the door and straight to his room and when we do talk he does it while he's strumming his guitar, and you have to talk to him over the chords. It's very funny but that's the way he is."

And that's just the way his fans like him.

Zayn, Harry, Liam, Louis, and Niall attend the *Men In Black 3* after party at the USS *Intrepid* on May 23, 2012.

Niall visits Six Flags on June 15, 2012, in Valencia, California.

Chapter 4:

VAIN ZAYN

Chapter 4:
VAIN ZAYN

Who would have guessed that Zayn Malik – Mr. Hair Gel himself – would be a bit of a momma's boy? That's right. This well-dressed, slightly moody musician still lets Mom, Tricia Brannan, do his laundry. Not all the time, of course. But she's more than happy to travel to London from her home in East Bowling, Bradford, just so Zayn has properly cleaned and folded undies.

"I don't expect Zayn to text me all the time, but I text him 'Night night son' and he texts back 'Love you mum,'" she told *The (London) Daily Mirror* in April 2012.

Tricia is so proud of Zayn that she's turned his childhood home into a bit of a shrine; photos of her son and the rest of One Direction are everywhere. And by "everywhere," we mean everywhere, from tea towels to cell phone covers.

"Zayn's mum has an enormous clock with his face as the background on their mantelpiece," a source told *The (London) Daily Star*. "In some ways it's really sweet, but in others it's a bit over the top."

Perhaps the put-her-son-on-a-pedestal act will die down after awhile; the fame game is still new for Zayn and his One Direction cohorts. For the most part, young Mr. Malik has led a fairly normal life.

Born January 12, 1993, in Bradford, West Yorkshire, England. His father, Yaser, is British Pakistani and his mother, Tricia, is English. He has an older sister, Doniya, and two younger sisters, Waliyha and Safaa.

Zayn grew up in an area south of Bradford city center. He says his mixed ethnicity initially made it difficult for him to fit in at school. He and Doniya attended several different schools before he ended up at Lower Fields Primary School in East Bowling and then Tong High School, a state comprehensive school.

As a kid, Zayn was shorter than most of his classmates and he recalls a few haircuts that were less than successful – including a couple times when he shaved his head and cut slits in his eyebrows for a rap/R&B-inspired look. He was not exactly "cool."

Then , when Zayn turned 12, things changed. He began to care about his appearance and admits to waking up an

WANT TO PUT A RING ON IT?

Thousands of girls dream of marrying Zayn Malik and it's not unusual for girls to stand at the gate outside his family house. But if you think getting his mom's attention is going to help your case, you can forget about it. "Fans ask me for permission to marry him," said Zayn's mom, Tricia Bannon, "but he can choose his own Mrs."

ABOUT ZAYN

Full name:	Zayn Jawaad Malik
Hometown:	West Lane Baildon, Bradford, England
Birthdate:	January 12, 1993
Astrological sign:	Capricorn
***The X Factor* audition song:**	"Let Me Love You"
Favorite American food:	Pretzels
Favorite book:	*Harry Potter*
Favorite Pokemon:	Oshawott
Celebrity crushes:	Actresses Megan Fox and Jessica Alba and singer Katy Perry
If there was a One Direction movie, actor who might portray him:	Canadian actor Avan Jogia (*Victorious*)
On Twitter:	@zaynmalik1D
Twitter followers:	4.56 million as of July 2012

Zayn performs at St. James Theatre on April 22, 2012, in Wellington, New Zealand.

Chapter 4:
VAIN ZAYN

hour before his sister just so he could style his hair. He dressed better, had a better attitude and, suddenly, girls began to notice him.

Zayn proudly sang in school choirs as he was growing up and he had roles in a couple of school musicals.

"I have quite a few videos of him singing as a little boy, but he's banned me from showing anyone. My favorite is him singing 'I Believe I Can Fly' wearing a green dressing gown," said his mother. "Zayn was always playing music on his computer and singing along to it for hours."

No matter how you look at it, it's a big leap from singing in your bedroom with the door locked to entering a nationwide, televised talent competition. But Zayn gathered his courage and did just that.

He attended the 2010 *X Factor* auditions in Manchester, England, singing a soulful version of Mario's "Let Me Love You." Without a second's hesitation, the show's judges gave him three "Yes" votes, sending him forward in the competition.

Zayn first came to the attention of *The X Factor* audience members when he refused to join other contestants on stage for a dance routine during the boot

MODERN-DAY VAN GOGH?

Everyone knows Zayn is a musical artist, but did you know he also has mad visual art talent too? He even received credit for some of the illustrations on One Direction's debut CD.

Apparently not everyone is a fan of Zayn's sketches, especially when he creates less-than-flattering doddles of his band mates.

"The other day I didn't draw Louis' hair the way I usually do it and he really moaned so I know exactly what annoys him," Zayn told *The (London) Sun*. "I can make them look really ugly — big cauliflower ears on Niall and a banana on Harry's head."

Sketch on, Zayn, sketch on.

SCHOOL DAZE

Zayn took to Twitter in August 2012 to let fans know that he actually misses school: *"@Farah907 school days are some of the best times of your life. Enjoy them, you'll miss them when you leave :) x"*

Perhaps that's not a surprising admission when you learn that - had fame not come his way - Zayn planned to attend college to become a teacher.

Zayn performs at the Bank Atlantic Center in Sunrise, Florida, on July 1, 2012.

GUIDE TO ZAYN'S TATTOOS

Zayn is a big fan of body art and he's happily adding to his collection at a fairly steady pace. In June 2012, the dark-haired heartthrob showed off his newest tattoo while performing on stage at the Gibson Amphitheatre in Los Angeles. The musically inspired design – a large microphone and cord on his right forearm – is an obvious tribute to his passion.

For those wondering about the rest of Zayn's ink, we offer this guide:

Botanical beauty: Located on the back of his neck, this intricate image of a silver fern is one of his newest body art additions. The silver fern is a lucky symbol in New Zealand.

Arabic inscriptions: There are two – count 'em, two – such messages. The words on his left collarbone mean "Be true to who you are." Zayn also has the Arabic version of his grandfather's name, Walter, tattooed on his chest.

Wrist work: Thought to be one of his first tattoos, Zayn has a small yin-yang symbol on his left wrist. This ancient symbol represents the Chinese understanding of how things work. The outer circle represents "everything," while the black and white shapes within the circle represent the interaction of two energies, called "yin" (black) and "yang" (white), which cause everything to happen.

Good fortunes: Zayn has a stylized image of crossed fingers etched onto his forearm. Zayn has said in many interviews that this tattoo is simply a good luck symbol.

In the cards: Is he a player? The playing card tattoo on Zayn's chest might lead you to believe so. Look closer, you'll see the card's design includes a crown with the initials "Z.M." on it.

The tats, they are a'changing: That Japanese symbol on his hip that reportedly meant lucky? It's gone – covered up with a heart symbol. Maybe Zayn decided he needed less luck and more love?

Zayn performs at St. James Theatre in Wellington, New Zealand, on April 22, 2012.

Zayn performs live at Gibson Amphitheatre on June 16, 2012, in Universal City, California.

ZAYN'S HOMETOWN

With nearly 300,000 residents, it should be no surprise that Bradford, England, has produced some notable folks in the world of arts and entertainment. These days, though, novelists and playwrights are taking a backseat to the city's new favorite son: Zayn Malik.

Bradford rose to prominence during the 19th century as an international center for the manufacture of textiles, quickly becoming known as the "wool capital of the world." The area's access to a supply of coal, iron ore and soft water spurred on its growth.

In recent years, the significance of manufacturing has declined, and tourism has taken on new importance. Bradford has become the first UNESCO City of Film with attractions such as the National Media Museum and the Alhambra Theatre. The area is home to several world-class art museums and Bradford City Park features a mirror pool as well as 100 fountains, laser lights and mist effects. The city also has a reputation for having some of the best Asian restaurants in the country.

As a teen living in the area, Zayn attended Tong High School, a multi-cultural, co-educational school for 11-19-year-olds. Approximately 1,600 students attend the state-of-the-art educational facility, which prides itself on the strength of its academic programs.

Among the region's most well-known residents are:

- **Sir Edward Appleton**, a physicist and Nobel prizewinner.
- Pop singer **Tasmin Archer**, whose first album, *Great Expectations*, yielded the hit "Sleeping Satellite" which reached No. 1 in the United Kingdom and Ireland.
- Author **John Braine**, who is chiefly remembered today for his first novel, *Room at the Top*, which was turned into a film by the same name.
- **Anne Bronte**, a British novelist and poet, the youngest member of the Bronte literary family.
- **Charlotte Bronte**, an English novelist and poet, the eldest of the three Bronte sisters who survived into adulthood. She wrote *Jane Eyre* under the pen name Currer Bell.
- **Emily Jane Bronte**, an English novelist and poet, best remembered for her novel, *Wuthering Heights*. She published under the pen name Ellis Bell.
- Author **Eric Knight**, who is mostly remembered for creating the fictional collie Lassie.
- **Adrian David Moorhouse**, a swimmer-turned-sports commentator who dominated British swimming in the late 1980s. He won the 100 meter breaststroke at the Seoul Olympics.
- **Robert Turner**, a pathologist who pioneered the use of chemotherapy in the treatment of cancer at the Bradford Royal Infirmary.

camp portion of the show. Celebrity judge and mentor Simon Cowell noticed his reluctance to participate and convinced him that, by not dancing, he was throwing away a tremendous opportunity. The pep talk worked; Zayn continued to compete and ultimately became one-fifth of one of the hottest musical acts of all time.

Looking back on it now, Zayn marvels at how it all worked out.

"I think we went into (*The X Factor*) competition just like anyone else who enters - to see how you'll do and not expecting anything really," he told *The (London) Sunday Mirror* in January 2012. "My whole reason in the first place was my mum who used to tell me I could sing, but I wanted to find out from someone else."

And find out he did. He and his band mates have become like brothers, performing together, sometimes living together and traveling together. While others in the group are pranksters or partiers, Zayn's reputation is that of "The Vain One." He admits to fussing over hair and clothes, often working to create looks that make it appear like he didn't fuss at all.

"Zayn is very quiet, but also pretty mental

Zayn performs on NBC's *Today* show at Rockefeller Plaza on March 12, 2012, in New York City.

Zayn attends a CD signing for *Up All Night* at Walmart on March 17, 2012, in Somerdale, New Jersey.

Chapter 4:
VAIN ZAYN

HOUSEWARMING GIFTS FOR ZAYN

Luxury vacations, jewelry, sports cars. Different stars spend their fortunes in different ways.

Zayn Malik has decided to sink some of his hard-earned cash into the real estate market. *The (London) Sun* reported in June 2012 that Zayn has spent a cool £2.2 million (roughly $3.4 million in U.S. dollars) on a home in Hyver Hill, a popular residential neighborhood in North London. The two-story detached dwelling is just a few blocks from the house where he and the guys stayed while competing on *The X Factor*.

The purchase came just a month after fire broke out in Zayn's swanky North London apartment; a friend had been staying in the flat to look after his dog.

"Everybody in the block had to evacuate the building," a source told HeatWorld.com. "One of the flats is completely gutted and a few have been badly damaged by smoke."

Thankfully, no one was hurt in that blaze. And, there's no indication that the incident played a role in Zayn's decision to become a homeowner.

The suave singer's new abode reportedly has six bedrooms and a separate "leisure complex" that includes an indoor swimming pool, sauna and changing rooms.

A source told *The Sun* that the pool was a huge selling point for the singer, who is already planning some parties for when the guys are all back in town. The house sits on a large, one-acre lot with beautifully landscaped gardens complete with its own secret garden and pond.

"Zayn is trying to be smart with his money by putting it into bricks and mortar," the source told the newspaper.

Zayn visits J&R Music and Computer World on March 12, 2012, in New York City.

and very random," band mate Liam Payne told STV in February 2012.

The handsome singer has come under occasional media attack for his smoking or inappropriate gestures or religion or drinking or very late-night partying. But, more than all of that combined, the media seems fascinated with his love life.

Of course, someone as good looking as Zayn has had many girlfriends, but this time it appears to be serious. ZM first dated Little Mix singer Perrie Edwards in fall 2011; the two rekindled their romance when he returned from his first U.S. tour in spring 2012.

Perrie's mom, Debbie Edwards, is supportive of the young stars' romance. She told *The (London) Sunday Sun*: "They make a lovely couple. I really hope they make a go of it. I've been to his house and met the two of them with his mum and his three sisters, and I think they're really good for each other."

The couple has publicly tweeted their love for each other (the social media version of shouting it to the world) and they insist that their busy tour schedules are helping - not hindering - the relationship.

Zayn performs live at the Beacon Theatre on May 26, 2012, in New York City.

Zayn attends the Sony after party for the 2012 BRIT awards at The Arts Club on February 21, 2012, in London, England.

"I'm really happy," Perrie told *The Sun*. "When you both do the same kind of thing, there's more understanding because you both get it... and it's more exciting when you see each other."

Other than having millions of young fans singing along to his songs and clamoring for tickets to his shows, oh, and having an equally famous girlfriend, Zayn insists his life hasn't changed much since his days back in Bradford. In fact, he's intent on staying true to his friends and family.

The star even makes time for an occasional visit to teachers and students at his old primary school.

FOOT FREAK

Two feet, four socks. Yes, you did the math correctly, that's two socks per foot. And that's the way Zayn likes it. No clue why the pop star likes to double up on his socks, but singer Manika, who joined One Direction on its U.S. tour, says this most abnormal habit is the norm for Zayn.

"Zayn Malik always wears two pairs of socks," she told *OK!* magazine, adding that he "even used to put a couple of pairs on as soon as he had jumped out of the swimming pool. Strange, but true."

Zayn visits ET Canada studios on March 26, 2012, in Toronto.

Zayn performs with a puppy from the Delco SPCA at radio station Q102 iHeartRadio Performance Theater in Bala Cynwyd, Pennsylvania.

Chapter 4:
VAIN ZAYN

"It's brilliant," the school's head master, John Edwards, told *The (Bradford) Telegraph & Argus* in March 2012. "The thing that impresses me about Zayn is that fame hasn't changed him one bit ... He is totally unaffected, respectful, a delightful young man. It couldn't have happened to a nicer person."

Zayn poses during a photo shoot at the Intercontinental Hotel on April 11, 2012, in Sydney, Australia.

Zayn performs on NBC's *Today* show at Rockefeller Plaza on March 12, 2012, in New York City.

Chapter 5:

LEVELHEADED LIAM

Chapter 5:
LEVELHEADED LIAM

There have been plenty of highlights along the way for the guys in 1D. But, for Liam Payne, none has compared to the band's March 2012 performance at Birmingham, England's, LG Arena.

Liam grew up just 12 miles away from Birmingham, in Wolverhampton. For him, this was a homecoming. For fans, it was a chance to see a local boy who'd made it to the big time.

"My audition in Birmingham was in the NEC (National Exhibition Centre at the LG Arena)," Liam told the *Birmingham Mail* in February 2012. "It's nice to come back and play those places and know that is where your career started off, and to play for the home crowd."

And right there, in that "home crowd" were Liam's parents, Geoff and Karen, and his two older sisters, Ruth and Nicola. His family has long been among his most ardent supporters.

Liam was born August 29, 1993, three weeks ahead of his due date. As an infant, he was quite fragile, suffering from a number of health problems. At one time, he was getting 32 injections in an arm each morning and evening. In the end, one of his kidneys was removed.

In spite of his health challenges – or, perhaps because of them – he became a bold and confident child. He first sang in public when he was five years old, performing a rendition of Robbie Williams' "Let Me Entertain You" in a holiday camp competition. His mother encouraged this creativity, often juggling her shifts as a nurse so that she could accompany him to lessons and auditions.

While still quite young, Liam and his sisters began taking classes at the Wolverhampton-based performing arts

WHAT A CROC!

Liam Payne feared a croc attack when the lads filmed their video for the song "Got to Be You."

The band made the video on New York's Lake Placid. While alligators and crocodiles aren't unheard of in New York state, they certainly are rare. In 2001, NYC was captivated by a caiman that eluded authorities in Central Park for a week. In 2003, cops caught a 4-foot croc that was wandering around a Queens park.

Said Liam: "There was a lake by our hotel and we went kayaking; when Niall turned the boat over I freaked because I thought I'd be eaten by a croc like in a movie."

Fortunately, no crocs appeared.

ABOUT LIAM

Full name:	Liam James Payne
Hometown:	Wolverhampton, England
Birthdate:	August 29, 1993
Astrological sign:	Virgo
***The X Factor* audition song:**	"Cry Me a River" in 2010, "Fly Me to the Moon" in 2008
Favorite American food:	Cheeseburgers
Favorite flicks:	*Click, Toy Story*
Favorite Pokemon:	Throh
Celebrity crush:	Reality TV star Kim Kardashian
If there was a One Direction movie, actor who might portray him:	American actor Zac Efron
On Twitter:	@Real_Liam_Payne
Twitter followers:	4.85 million as of July 2012

Liam attends the *Men In Black 3* New York Premiere at Ziegfeld Theatre on May 23, 2012, in New York City.

school Pink Productions, where he is remembered as a timid boy who had natural ability and charisma.

"Who'd have thought the Liam we see today would have nearly had to be forced onto the stage?" instructor Jodie Richards told the *Birmingham Mail* in October 2010. "It was clear very early that Liam was a natural talent. He gained more and more confidence with each show and took on some big singing numbers."

Liam was also heavily

SERENADING SHOPPERS

The next time you see someone busking on a street corner or outside the subway, you might want to give him a double take. It could be someone famous.

One Direction's Liam and Niall stunned shoppers at the Westfield retail centre in London in early August 2012, when the two set up a makeshift stage near an escalator and started performing.

Shoppers quickly realized the buskers were two of their favorite 1D members and gathered around to watch them perform an acoustic version of the group's biggest hits, including "What Makes You Beautiful."

No word on how much change the two collected in their open guitar case.

Liam attends the *Big Time Movie* New York premiere at 583 Park Avenue on March 8, 2012, in New York City.

LIAM'S HOMETOWN

Liam is a Yam Yam. Really.

His hometown of Wolverhampton has such a long name that locals often call it Wolvo or W'ton or even Wolves. The people from W'ton? They're known as Wulfrunians or, colloquially, as Yam Yams.

All that's fine with Liam, who considers the city a fine place to grow up.

Wolverhampton is located in the West Midlands, England. In 2004, the local government district had an estimated population of 239,100. The surrounding metropolitan area had a population of 2.3 million, making it the second largest urban area in the United Kingdom. Wolverhampton is just 17 miles from Birmingham, England.

The city got its start as a market town, specializing in the wool trade. During and after the Industrial Revolution, the city became a major industrial center; many residents worked in mining as well as in the production of steel, locks, motorcycles and cars. Today, Wolverhampton boasts a vibrant mix of business, shopping, art, theatre, sport and nightlife.

Liam was a music technology student at the City of Wolverhampton College. Before *The X Factor,* he had once performed in front of a 26,000 crowd at a Wanderers' football match. (No wonder, then, that the Wanderers are his favorite sports team.)

Visitors to Wolverhampton have many attractions and activities from which to choose. The city has fine art and craft museums, beautiful gardens and concert halls. The Wolverhampton Grand Theatre was opened in 1894, where a young Charlie Chaplin was a company call boy in 1902. Wightwick Manor and Gardens is one of the city's most popular tourist attractions; the estate features extraordinary collections of William Morris wallpaper, pre-Raphaelite art and De Morgan pottery.

Sports fans who visit the area can enjoy football at Molineux Stadium, home of the Wolverhampton Wanderers, or spend a day at the races – horses, greyhounds or autos.

In 2009, the renowned Lonely Planet guide named Wolverhampton the "fifth worst city on the globe." City officials fought back, claiming no one from the Lonely Planet had even been to Wolverhampton before adding it to the list.

Malcolm Gwinnett, deputy mayor of Wolverhampton, told *The Mail*: "The people who have come up with this list obviously don't have a clue what they are talking about.

"Wolverhampton is a lovely place to live in many parts. It has its downsides just like any other city, but over the past ten years, whoever has been in charge of the city has pushed it forward."

Perhaps Yam Yam Liam's superstar status will, in some small way, improve his hometown's image.

Liam performs with One Direction in New York on Saturday, May 26, 2012. (AP Photo/Charles Sykes)

Chapter 5: LEVELHEADED LIAM

involved in sports and tried out for various school teams. He excelled at running and found his place on the cross country team. He routinely woke up at 6:00 in the morning to go for long training runs. By the time he was 12, he was fast enough that coaches awarded him a spot on the under-18 team.

Also around the time he turned 12, Liam joined a boxing gym. He put his boxing skills to good use, fending off bullies in secondary school.

Liam came into *The X Factor* competition with considerably more experience than his fellow band members. He was studying musical technology in college at the time and had done a number of regional performances.

He'd also auditioned for the show in 2008, making it to the portion of competition where contestants are mentored at the judges' houses. Though the rejection stung, Liam now sees the wisdom in the judges' decision.

"I was too young," he told the *Birmingham Mail* in February 2012.

Liam could have been defeated by his early elimination from the show but, instead, he worked to improve, learning to control and strengthen his voice.

It took a lot of courage for Liam to head back to auditions two years later, but he did.

His 2010 audition, in which he performed "Cry Me a River," earned a standing ovation from Simon Cowell and "Yes" votes from all four of the show's judges.

"That was really impressive – really, really impressive," said judge Natalie Imbruglia. "I think other people in this competition should be a little bit worried about you. You're really good – really."

"I'm really glad you came back. That was a brilliant, brilliant vocal," agreed judge Louis Walsh. "And for 16 years (of age) – it was so confident; you totally delivered."

Liam was happily working his way

LIAMS ALL AROUND

Liam's name, which means "will, desire and protection," fits him well. It's a name that has become increasingly popular in recent years: In 2011, it was the 15th most popular boy's name in the United States and the 33rd most popular in the United Kingdom.

Other celebrity Liams include actors Liam Neeson (*Unknown, Wrath of the Titans, Taken*), Liam Aiken (*A Series of Unfortunate Events, Stepmom*), Liam Cunningham (*Clash of the Titans, Game of Thrones*), and musicians Liam Finn (indie rock) and Liam Gallagher (formerly of the band Oasis, currently with Beady Eye).

Liam makes a surprise visit to Westfield London Shopping Centre on August 2, 2012, in England.

Chapter 5:
LEVELHEADED LIAM

DANCING WITH THE STAR

In this case, Liam is the celebrity and his girlfriend, Danielle Peazer, is the professional dancer. The leggy brunette is a dancer for bands including The Saturdays, JLS, LMFAO and singer Jessie J. The couple met when Liam appeared on *The X Factor* in 2010.

through the various stages of the competition when once again he was cut. This time, though, he and four other guys (Niall, Louis, Harry and Zayn) were offered a second chance if they were willing to perform together as a band.

The group's mentor, Simon Cowell, said he had positive feelings about the guys from the moment the five of them were called back onto the stage to hear the judges' offer.

"The minute they stood there for the first time together – it was a weird feeling," Cowell told *Rolling Stone* in April 2012. "They just looked like a group at that point."

Liam was considerably less confident as the guys struggled through their initial meetings and rehearsals. "My first thought was, 'Are we going to make this work when we don't know each other?' It was such a leap of faith," he said,

"The first few days were quite tough," he told the *South Wales Echo*. "We all had

THE HAIRCUT SEEN ROUND THE WORLD

Singer Justin Bieber made headlines when he trimmed his trademark mop top around the time he turned 18. And Liam has done the same thing.

In August 2012, just before his 19th birthday, Liam ditched his long locks for a shorter, more mature cut worthy of countless news articles and magazine photos.

When at home, Liam gets his hair cut at Royston Blythe Hair Salon, owned by Nick Malenko. Though he didn't go there for the "big" shear, Malenko was complimentary of Liam's new style.

"Liam has a great face so he can't really go wrong with his hair," he said.

Liam performs at Hordern Pavilion on April 13, 2012, in Sydney, Australia.

SAY NO TO SOLO

Liam Payne has said he has no intention of ever going it alone - labeling a solo career as "massively boring."

Liam and the guys – Harry, Louis, Niall and Zayn – all originally auditioned for *The X Factor* in 2010 as solo artists but judges put them together as a group during the competition. Apparently that "team spirit" is something Liam has grown fond of.

In an August 2012 interview with *The (London) Sun*, Liam dismissed the idea of becoming a solo act.

"I think it would be massively, massively boring," he said. "I don't know how Justin Bieber does it, but full props to him. I like being around the boys. I enjoy other people's company and it's a lot more fun being in a band on stage."

Hmmmm. Only time will tell. Many former band members have gone on to very successful and, presumably, happy careers. A few of the most notable:

- Beyonce, who performed with Destiny's Child
- Phil Collins, who performed with Genesis
- Gloria Estefan, who performed with The Miami Sound Machine
- Peter Gabriel, who performed with Genesis
- Don Henley, who performed with The Eagles
- Lauryn Hill, who performed with The Fugees
- Billy Idol, who performed with Generation X
- Michael Jackson, who performed with The Jackson 5
- John Lennon, who performed with The Beatles
- Ricky Martin, who performed with Menudo
- Paul McCartney, who performed with The Beatles
- George Michael, who performed with Wham
- Diana Ross, who performed with The Supremes
- Gwen Stefani, who performed with No Doubt
- Sting, who performed with The Police
- Justin Timberlake, who performed with 'N Sync

Liam performs live at St. James Theatre on April 22, 2012, in Wellington, New Zealand.

different ideas but we didn't really know what a group was about."

As the guys began to mesh, they quickly attracted a huge television following and fan base. It was an incredible now-or-never kind of experience.

"Normally when you put together a band they have some time to go away and develop, but we had to do that in a live competition in front of 20 million people,"

Liam plays with the microphone during an interview with Alan Jones on April 11, 2012, in Sydney, Australia.

Liam performs at Trusts Stadium on April 21, 2012, in Auckland, New Zealand.

Chapter 5:
LEVELHEADED LIAM

Liam said. "If you make a mistake in front of an audience like that, you get voted out. We had no room for error whatsoever. We had to grow up very, very fast."

Sure, the guys still act like, well, guys. But Liam is happy to fill the role as the group's "smart and sensible" one.

"I often get described as Papa Smurf," he told STV in February 2012.

As One Direction's fame grows, Liam

Liam visits J&R Music and Computer World on March 12, 2012, in New York City.

Liam visits J&R Music and Computer World on March 12, 2012, in New York City.

and his band mates are adjusting to the demands of touring, recording, and making appearances. He's also learning that fans and the media have an intense desire to learn every little detail about his life, such as what he looks for in a girl and his irrational fear of restaurant spoons.

The media has been especially hot-on-the-trail of the story of Liam's love life. Photos and stories – often fabricated – about his romance with dancer Danielle Peazer have found their way into newspapers and fan mags for as long as the two have been together. In summer 2012, rumors began circulating that Liam and Danielle were set to get married – a report One Direction spokespeople have adamantly denied.

Liam also denied the engagement rumors, taking to Twitter to set the record straight. He directly called out the newspaper and reporter (Gordon Smart) who first reported the non-news: *"I'm not getting married the Sun newspaper can't seem to wait for me to get married. Gordon no need to rush. When I am I'll send u an invite."*

Two years ago, Liam could not have imagined that rumors about his love life would make international news or that he'd become one fifth of the hottest boy band around.

"We never expected any of this at all," Liam told Radio City. "We thought that we would do a little bit in the U.K. after the end of the show. Now it has gone all over the world and more things have happened to us than we would ever have imagined."

Liam attends the Sony after party for the 2012 BRIT awards at The Arts Club in London England.

Liam visits ET Canada Studios on March 26, 2012, in Toronto.

Chapter 6:

HARRY THE LADIES MAN

Chapter 6:
HARRY THE LADIES MAN

Harry Styles is a charmer – and has been from the very beginning.

Born February 1, 1994, in Holmes Chapel, Chesire, England, his mother Ann Cox told *The People* (London): "Ever since he was little, he has made people smile. I always thought he'd end up on the stage. He always loved attention and making people laugh. He's certainly not been shy about himself."

Harry's father, Des, recalled a vacation to Cypress when crowds of 16- and 17-year-old girls flocked around his nine-year-old son, expressing their love for the much-younger man.

"He's just got this fantastic, personable demeanor to him. Clearly he's a bit special," Des told *The (Scotland) Daily Record* in June 2012. "It's not just his looks but he's very charming, it's like a gift really. I always knew he'd succeed at whatever he did because he'd always charm people, from performing in the car or on holiday, he'd always be able to hold a crowd or hold a room even when he was a kid."

Harry was a very happy child, recalled his dad. Perhaps that's why Des is still troubled by the memory of having to tell Harry and his sister, Gemma, that he was leaving the children's mother.

"He was only about seven when I sat them down and told them I was leaving," Des told *The Daily Record*. "Everybody was in tears. We were sitting in the lounge. Gemma and Harry were sitting on the floor in front of us, Anne and I on the sofa, and both of them were crying. Generally, you wouldn't see him cry as much as maybe some kids do – he wasn't ·generally emotional or a cry baby – but he cried then.

"The way we sat them down and told them we weren't going to be together anymore; it was probably the worst day of my life.

"I didn't just leave, it was a decision

AN IDOL'S IDOL

You might think the super famous are above having idols. Not true.

In a 2012 interview on Tumblr's Storyboard, Harry confessed his love for Chris Martin as a singer and said he'd like to emulate him.

"My biggest idol has always been Chris Martin from Coldplay," he said. "He is such a great singer, performer and writer. If I could be as talented as any musician, it would be him all day long."

When Sugar Scape asked Martin about Harry's adoration, he be began giggling.

"Did he really say that?" The Coldplay singer asked. "I'm getting all... blushing!"

ABOUT HARRY

Full name:	Harry Edward Styles
Hometown:	Holmes Chapel, Cheshire, England
Birthdate:	February 1, 1994
Astrological sign:	Aquarius
The X Factor **audition song:**	"Isn't She Lovely"
Favorite American food:	Beef jerky
Favorite flicks:	*Love Actually, Fight Club*
Favorite Pokemon:	Sauk
Celebrity crushes:	American actress Blake Lively, English pop and R&B singer Frankie Sandford
If there was a One Direction movie, actor who might portray him:	British actor Orlando Bloom
On Twitter:	@Harry_Styles
Twitter followers:	5.57 million as of July 2012

we should split," Des said, recalling those heartbreaking days. "Things weren't good for a while but it was the best way forward. At the time, everybody was in tears but children are very resilient."

Resiliency did win out. Harry and Gemma continued to live with their mother who remarried. Though separated by distance, Des continued to support his children financially and emotionally, and made time

Harry performs at Hisense Arena on April 16, 2012, in Melbourne, Australia.

Harry stops to pose while at BBC Radio One on August, 10, 2011, in London, England.

to see them every few weeks.

Perhaps buoyed by adversity, Harry turned to music. He practiced singing on a karaoke machine his grandfather bought him and participated in school plays at Holmes Chapel Comprehensive School.

"The first time I sang in a school production, I got a rush that was something I really enjoyed and wanted to do more of," Harry told *The People*.

Harry attends a CD signing for *Up All Night* at Walmart on March 17, 2012, in Somerdale, New Jersey.

HARRY'S HOMETOWN

Handsome Harry Styles grew up in Holmes Chapel, a village located in Cheshire, England.

The 2001 census reported the population of the village as 5,669. The town, which is located about 175 miles from London, has a railway station which provides services to Manchester and Crew.

Also known as Church Hulme, this parish originally was called Hulme, derived from Hulm or Holm, meaning rising ground.

The village has a small shopping district, grocery store, hardware store, library, several pubs, a pizzeria and a fish and chips shop.

Harry, himself, has described his hometown as "boring."

"There's nothing much happens there ... it's quite picturesque," he said in his behind-the-scenes interviews on *The X Factor*.

One of the area's most picturesque attractions is the Swettenham Meadows nature preserve, located about 2.5 miles east of Holmes Chapel. The 21-acre grassland preserve is rich with common spotted orchids, marsh orchids, many species of butterflies, kingfishers and amphibians.

While living in this sleepy community, Harry attended Holmes Chapel Comprehensive School, and as a teen he worked Saturdays at the town bakery, W Mandeville.

During Harry's stint on *The X Factor*, his coworkers showed their support by painting messages on the bakery windows, urging the entire village to vote for their native son.

In a 2010 interview with the *Crewe Chronicle*, W Mandeville owner Simon Wakefield said Harry would be welcome to come back to the bakery to work at any time – though he doubted that would happen.

"I think his career is sorted," he said. "He is a great lad and was really popular with the customers when he used to work on counter."

Chapter 6:
HARRY THE LADIES MAN

In England, students ages 14-16 take exams in a number of subject areas to earn their General Certificate of Secondary Education (GCSE). Harry was studying for his exams and working part time in a bakery when his band, White Eskimo, won a battle of the bands competition.

"I got such a thrill when I was in front of that many people singing," he said. "It really showed me that's what I wanted to do."

Harry performs at Hordern Pavilion on April 13, 2012, in Sydney, Australia.

Harry attends the *Men In Black 3* New York premiere at Ziegfeld Theatre on May 23, 2012.

THE MANY LOVES OF HARRY STYLES

Handsome Harry Styles has been linked to a good number of women over the course of his red-hot career – several of them significantly older than he is. Among the ladies with whom he's (reportedly) been snuggling:

Caggie Dunlop

Harry and Caggie were quick to deny rumors they were romantically linked but the two sure looked cozy when photographers snapped them in June 2012 in Dosia, a West London night club.

After the pair were spotted together, a source told the *(London) Daily Mirror* that the two had been flirting even before One Direction headed to the United States for their first tour.

The source said: "It was obvious Harry had a bit of a thing for Caggie because he started tweeting her before they had ever even met. And when they actually saw each other in person, they hit it off straight away. There was obviously real chemistry between them."

Singer and actress Dunlop is best known as the former star of the partially scripted reality TV show *Made in Chelsea*. The young actress studied at the Lee Strasberg Theatre and Film Institute in New York City. Her family home is located on the Isle of Wight, but she spends most of her time in London.

Caroline Flack

Harry's three-month romance with 32-year-old Caroline Flack ended in January 2012. The relationship sparked controversy largely because of their big age difference.

Harry's father, Des, was openly opposed to his son's relationship with Flack, telling *People* magazine he thought the age gap was "ridiculous."

"Thirty-two (or) whatever she was and Harry 17," he said, "That's a bit extreme."

Flack is an English television personality, best known for presenting *I'm a Celebrity ... Get Me Out of Here! Now!* from 2008 to 2010.

Lucy Horobin

The (London) Sunday Mirror reported in June 2012 that the amorous One Direction singer enjoyed a relationship with radio DJ Lucy Horobin, who is 14 years his senior – and who was married at the time.

The newspaper reported that Harry met Horobin when his band appeared on her radio show in August 2011.

A friend of Horobin's told the paper: "He's adorable and Lucy had a lot of fun. But it was never anything serious. It was a mistake."

A source close to Harry told *The Sunday Mirror*: "Lucy was right up his street, exactly the type of girl, or woman, should I say, he is attracted to. She's sexy, confident, and is doing well in her career. But he never wanted anything serious."

Horobin, originally from Canterbury, England, attended Nottingham Trent

University where she achieved a degree in broadcast journalism.

Emily Atack

Breaking out of his pattern of dating much older women, Harry reportedly began a relationship with actress Emily Atack in May 2012; she is just four years older than the One Direction singer. The two reportedly dated for a very short time.

Atack, a former *Dancing on Ice* contestant, is best known for her role on the award-winning TV show *The Inbetweeners* and for posing for a number of well-known men's magazines. She's a London native.

Other ladies?

Harry's not at all shy when it comes to talking about women with whom he'd like to make a love connection. He's admitted a crush on former ABC *Bachelorette* Jillian Harris. (*US Magazine* reports that, when they met in Los Angeles in April 2012, Harry asked for Harris' number and she politely declined.)

He's also expressed an interested in connecting with singer Rihanna.

In April 2012, Rihanna told *The (London) Daily Mirror* that Harry caught her attention when she saw videos of One Direction.

Harry's reaction? "That is absolutely incredible – do we know where she is? I'd love to hook up. This is the best thing."

Harry performs at Hordern Pavilion on April 13, 2012, in Sydney, Australia.

Chapter 6:
HARRY THE LADIES MAN

The boy who was known for singing in the school corridors summoned his courage and showed up – along with thousands of other hopefuls – for the 2010 *X Factor* auditions in Chesire, England. Friends and family members accompanied the young singer, many of whom wore T-shirts emblazoned with the phrase "We Think Harry Has the X Factor." For his part, the curly-haired teen wowed judges with his rendition of Stevie Wonder's "Isn't She Lovely."

Once the show decided to put Harry into a band with fellow competitors Niall, Liam, Louis and Zayn, the five guys continued to impress. As time passed, they produced harmonies that were more and more impressive. Thanks to the televised competition, their fan base grew exponentially. Even though they didn't win their season of *The X Factor*, Harry and the fellows in One Direction have emerged as the show's most successful act – ever.

As the band's popularity has increased, so has the number of paparazzi tracking the musicians' every move. Harry, who has a reputation as the group's biggest flirt, has attracted considerable media attention. Most of the headlines focus on one of two topics: His tousled brown curls or his attraction to older (occasionally married) women.

Harry's father said he's done his part to warn his son about the dangers of getting involved with girls who now throw

INKED UP

Those keeping a close eye on Harry's body (and who isn't?) know that he's long had a large star tattoo on his inner arm. In summer 2012, he added the Temper Trap song lyrics "Won't stop 'til we surrender" beneath it.

In July 2012, the singer added another tattoo: a tiny letter "A" in the crook of his elbow. It's believed that the initial is a tribute to his mother Anne Cox, with whom Harry is very close.

DREAMER

Everybody dreams – even pop stars. Harry tells *The (London) Sun*, that his dreams are just as normal as the next guy's.

"I had a dream that I woke up in math...I've never had a dream where I felt famous," Harry confessed.

Harry performs at the St. James Theatre on April 22, 2012, in Wellington, New Zealand.

LOCKS OF LOVELINESS

Curls, glorious curls – they're a big part of heartthrob Harry Styles' appeal. In fact, styling product manufacturer Brylcreem named the 1D singer's 'do "Best Celebrity Hair" in 2010.

Sometimes Harry wears his curls loose and bouncy. Other times, the sexy singer goes for a more unkempt look – still full of body but less refined.

One of the reasons folks adore Harry's hairstyle is that it's not something everyone can wear. Even those with natural curl need a specific, longer cut and holding products to maintain the look.

The experts at Coolmenshair.com suggest that guys with thicker and slightly wavy locks may mimic Harry's trendy style by getting a sharp cut in order to enhance the natural curl; cutting down on extra weight will soften curls. Hair should be washed with specific curl enhancing products which will contribute to a softer appearance. Once the product has been worked into the locks, hair should be rough dried with a hairdryer on a low strength and then allowed to finish drying naturally.

Harry's well aware of the power of his tresses, so he's made a conscious decision to cut back on the amount of product he uses on his hair.

"I am a little concerned I might go bald soon," he told *The Sun*. "It worries me it might fall out. I am just watching how much I put on it now."

Of course, Harry is not the only superstar with luscious locks. Other male celebrities who rock the curls include:

- **Adrian Grenier,** an American actor, musician and director best known for his role on the HBO series *Entourage*.
- **Colin Firth**, an English film, television and theatre actor who won an Oscar in 2011 for his portrayal of King George VI in *The King's Speech*.
- **Jesse Eisenberg**, an American actor who has had roles in movies including *The Emperor's Club, The Squid and the Whale* and *The Social Network*.
- **Josh Groban**, a multi-platinum-selling American singer, song writer and record producer.
- **Matthew McConaughey**, an American actor best known for his roles in romantic comedies including *The Wedding Planner, How to Lose a Guy in 10 Days, Failure to Launch* and *Ghosts of Girlfriends Past*.
- **Matthew Morrison,** an American actor, dancer, musician and singer-songwriter, who gained fame on Broadway and for his role as Will Schuester on the FOX television show *Glee*.
- **Nick Jonas,** a singer-songwriter and actor best known for his role in the Jonas Brothers, an American pop-

rock band.

- **Sacha Baron Cohen**, an English comedian and actor known for characters including *Borat* and *The Dictator*.
- **Simon Baker**, an Australian actor and director who is best known for his lead role in the CBS TV series *The Mentalist*.
- **Will Ferrell**, an American comedian, actor and writer who has starred in films including *Old School, Elf, Anchorman, Talladega Nights, Semi-Pro* and *The Campaign*.

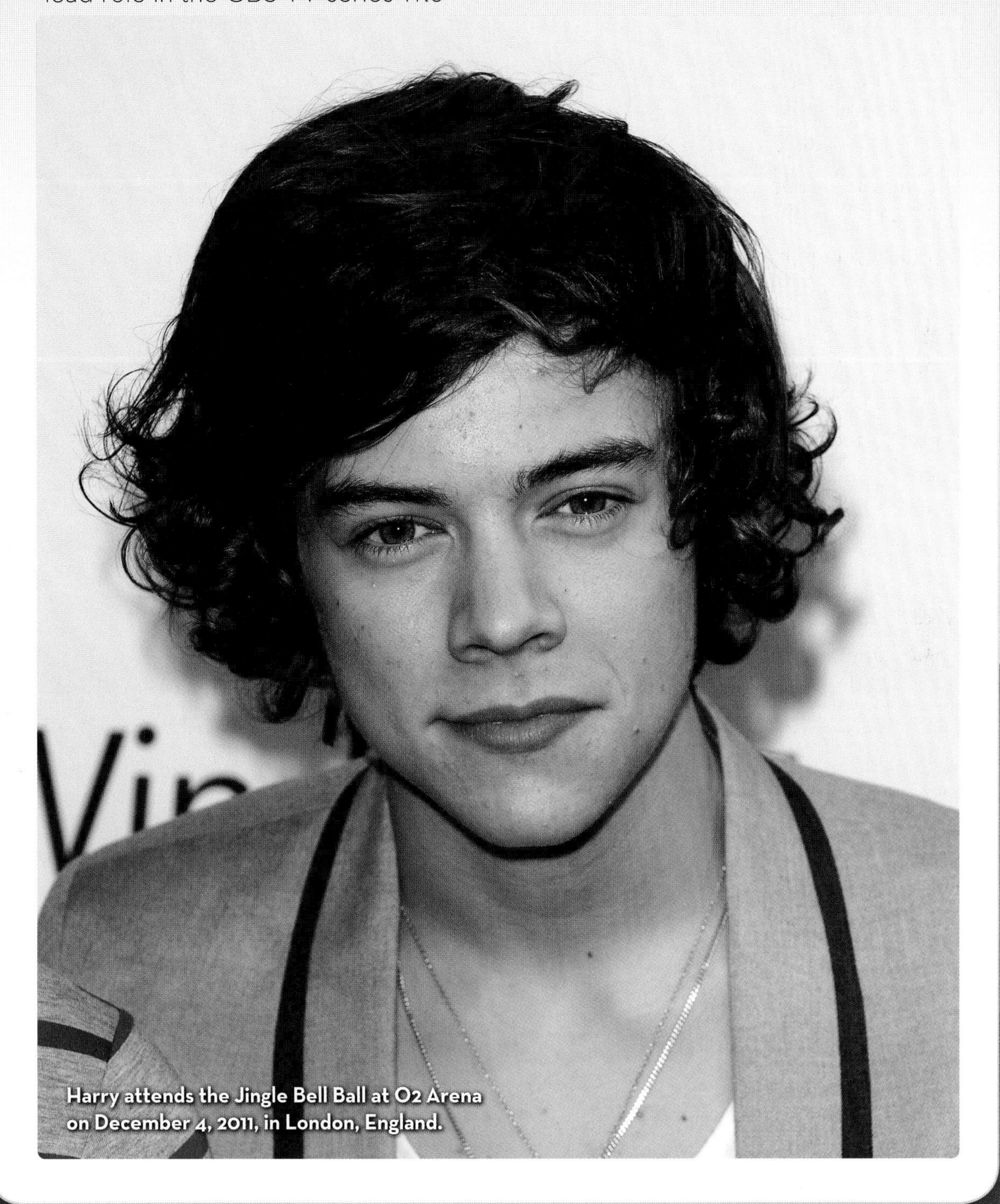

Harry attends the Jingle Bell Ball at O2 Arena on December 4, 2011, in London, England.

Chapter 6:
HARRY THE LADIES MAN

themselves at him.

"I never needed to sit him down and tell him about the birds and the bees. I tried to train him up as we went along," Des told *The Daily Record*. "We had those conversations and it was almost as though he'd say, 'Yeah, dad, I'm on board with that,' rather than going all sicky and saying, 'Oh dad don't talk about things like that,' you know the way some kids do. I said to

Harry performs at St. James Theatre on April 22, 2012, in Wellington, New Zealand.

Harry visits J&R Music and Computer World on March 12, 2012, in New York City.

Chapter 6:
HARRY THE LADIES MAN

Harry, 'Just make sure you don't get anyone pregnant because if that were to happen, it would really screw things up big time.'"

Harry understands that he's now living his life in the spotlight – and that it's just part of the price of doing what he loves. There are times, though, when fans (or reporters) cross the line.

In July 2012, for instance, a fan got a copy of Harry's birth certificate (a public record, so anyone can obtain it) and posted it on Twitter. The image was then retweeted by a One Direction Twitter news feed, all of which angered Harry's mom who considered the whole episode an invasion of privacy.

The same month, the pop star tried to visit his family's home in Chesire. He was mobbed by dozens of fans who surrounded his vehicle and chased him to his parents' property.

"He was furious," a source told *The London Sun*. "He doesn't mind signing autographs but when he can't get in his front door, it is ridiculous."

According to *The Sun*, Harry's devotees became such a nuisance that his family had to leave the property until Harry went back to his apartment in London. "It's not fair for neighbors to have random girls standing outside their houses 24/7," explained the source.

Rabid mobs are the exception, admitted Harry, who said he's thrilled by fans who show up at concerts wearing homemade T-shirts or carrying posters and banners. Those are the sorts of personal touches that show a genuine effort to connect with the band.

"In Boston, we did a meet-and-greet and these five girls came dressed as each of us," Harry told *The (London) Daily Mirror*. "They do that a lot. It's cool."

Harry's dad understands that fame comes with its frustrations, but he hopes his son continues to ride the wave as long as he can – even though that means he's often forced to keep up with his famous son via email and social media.

"The downside for me is I hardly see him," said Des. "But on Father's Day, Harry sent me texts saying 'Love you more than all the world, kiss kiss kiss,' from L.A. ... I'm just very proud to be his dad but I don't want to exploit that either, I just want to be here if he needs me."

Harry attends a CD signing for *Up All Night* at Walmart on March 17, 2012, in Somerdale, New Jersey.

Harry performs on NBC's *Today* show at Rockefeller Plaza on March 12, 2012, in New York City.

Chapter 7:

LOUIS THE PRANKSTER

Chapter 7:
LOUIS THE PRANKSTER

It was the car ride Louis Tomlinson's mom, Johannah, will never forget.

She was driving Louis' sisters around town when they heard on the radio that One Direction had scored its first No. 1 hit. The band's single "What Makes You Beautiful" had just topped the download chart. The group's hit had also broken Sony's record for the highest numbers of pre-orders, despite the record label owning top talents including Beyonce and Michael Jackson.

"I was driving, picking up Louis' sisters, when we heard they were the download number one. We were all just screaming," Johannah told the *Doncaster (England) Free Press* in September 2011.

Louis' family celebrated that milestone with a party – a really, really big party. Even Louis' great-grandma, Olive Rothery, came by to cheer the lad's success.

"She's 89, but she knows all the words to their song already and sings along," Johanna told the *Free Press*. "She's learned about the Internet to see what's on there about him."

Mom and great-grandma have long suspected Louis was destined for greatness.

ALL A'TWITTER

Louis spoke out via Twitter when singer Rebecca Ferguson dumped her management, accusing them of overworking her.

'@RebeccaFMusic Success is impossible without proper hard work.'

Perhaps realizing it was a mistake to voice his opinion in such a public way, the tweet was deleted – but not before Rebecca saw it. She replied:

'I forgive u. I used to be scared and think I had to do whatever they told me to do to.'

Her tweet also mysteriously disappeared.

BEST BOYFRIEND EVER!

Lucky Eleanor Calder!

Not only is she Louis' girlfriend, she also received one of the most amazing gifts a girl could ask for.

In honor of her 20th birthday on July 16, 2012, Louis asked one of Eleanor's favorite singers, Rihanna, to record a special birthday message for her. Rihanna complied, performing a personalized version of the "Happy Birthday" song.

ABOUT LOUIS

Full name:	Louis William Tomlinson
Hometown:	Doncaster, South Yorkshire, England
Birthdate:	December 24, 1991
Astrological sign:	Capricorn
***The X Factor* audition song:**	"Hey There Delilah"
Favorite American food:	Corn Pops cereal
Favorite Pokemon:	Pansear
Celebrity crush:	English singer/actress Cheryl Cole
If there was a One Direction movie, actor who might portray him:	British singer/songwriter Joe Brooks
On Twitter:	@Louis_Tomlinson
Twitter followers:	4.80 million as of July 2012

FANS: PLEASE SCREAM QUIETER!

Screams at One Direction concerts have reportedly reached 104 decibels. That's louder than a jet at takeoff.

Is it any wonder, then, that 1D's Louis has revealed that persistent screaming from the band's dedicated fans has left him partially deaf in one ear?

Louis revealed in August 2012 that he's suffered repeated headaches as a result of the noise. Shortly before headlining at Liverpool's Radio City Live, he said: "I am going slightly deaf in my right ear. It's tinnitus… something like that."

Louis has not officially been diagnosed with tinnitus, but he does exhibit many of the symptoms. Simply put, tinnitus is the perception of sound in the head, where no external source is present. Some call it "ringing in the ears" or "head noise."

Dr. Neil Cherian, a practicing otoneurologist at the Cleveland Clinic and director of its Center for Performance Medicine, is an expert when it comes to tinnitus.

"Professional musicians are in a difficult position since they rely on their ears for their livelihood, and they expose their ears to the rigors of their work," Cherian said. "For many musicians, tinnitus can be considered a repetitive strain injury."

Among the many musicians who suffer – or who have suffered – from the ailment are Eric Clapton, Barbra Streisand, Bob Dylan, Ozzy Osborne, Huey Lewis, Bono, Chris Martin and Phil Collins. Composer Ludwig van Beethoven is also thought to have suffered from tinnitus.

Concerned One Direction managers now insist that Louis and the rest of the band wear protective earpieces when on stage and during all rehearsals.

A source close to 1D told *The (London) Daily Mirror*: "Screams during gigs have started affecting the boys on stage. They are only young and still developing, so management insist they wear hi-tech earpieces and filters to reduce the volume of the screaming and the music."

Louis performs with One Direction at the SiriusXM studio on March 16, 2012, in New York City.

Chapter 7:
LOUIS THE PRANKSTER

The pop star-to-be was born December 24, 1991, in Doncaster, South Yorkshire, England, to mother Johannah Poulston and father Troy Austin. His parents divorced when he was young and he took the name of his stepfather, Mark Tomlinson. He has five younger stepsiblings.

Two of his stepsisters, Daisy and Phoebe, had roles as babies on *Fat Friends*, a television drama about a group of people

Louis looks on from the sideline during the ANZAC match between the New Zealand Kiwis and the Australian Kangaroos at Eden Park on April 20, 2012, in Auckland, New Zealand.

LOUIS' HOMETOWN

Olympic sailor Anna Tunnicliffe, heavyweight boxing champ Bruce Woodcock, and actress Kelly Harrison all have something important in common with 1D singer Louis Tomlinson: Their hometown.

Louis was born in Doncaster, a town in South Yorkshire, England, about 160 miles from London. Approximately 290,000 people live in "Donny" and its neighboring villages.

Coal and its transport played an important role in Doncaster's industrial history. As the economy changes and the coal industry declines, Doncaster leaders are still struggling to define its future. Consequently, unemployment in the area is higher than in other parts of the country.

Doncaster is a historic market town, founded in AD 71 by the Romans due to its strategic position on the River Don. The city sits at the heart of a vast metropolitan area, consisting of green open spaces and nature reserves.

Doncaster residents love their sporting events – particularly horse racing. The region's first horse track was established in 1615 and the Doncaster Cup horse race was first run in 1766, making it the oldest regulated horse race in the world. The sports of soccer, rugby, cricket, polo, golf and clay pigeon shooting also have many fans in the area.

Each year, thousands of tourists flock to Doncaster. Some of their most popular destinations are: Brockholes Farm, a combination riding school, zoo and working farm; Doncaster Museum and Art gallery; Doncaster Lakeside shopping center, and Aeroventure, an air museum based on the former site of wartime RAF Doncaster.

While growing up in Doncaster, Louis attended both Hall Cross and Hayfield schools; at Hall Cross, he starred in several musical productions.

Prior to finding fame and fortune as one-fifth of One Direction, Louis held down several part-time jobs in his hometown, including one at the Vue Cinema and another as a waiter in the hospitality suites at the Doncaster Rovers' football stadium.

Louis visits Six Flags Magic Mountain on June 15, 2012, in Valencia, California.

who use their body weight as an excuse for their failings. When the girls worked, Louis often went along and served as an extra. That tiny taste of performing whetted his interest. He began attending an acting school in Barnsley and earned bit parts in ITV's film *If I Had You* and BBC's *Waterloo Road*.

Louis' many activities meant he missed a lot of school – enough, in fact, that he failed

Louis performs with One Direction at HMV Hammersmith Apollo on January 22, 2011, in London, England.

Louis visits *The Elvis Duran Z100 Morning Show* in New York City for a pre-taped interview.

A BIT OF BRITISH COOKING

Louis has thoroughly enjoyed touring the world with One Direction but says he misses British food when he's on the road. Now, whenever he travels abroad, he takes Yorkshire tea along so he has a taste of home nearby. What other British delicacies might he be missing?

Yorkshire Pudding – This dish is not usually eaten as a dessert like other puddings but instead is part of the main course. Yorkshire pudding is made from flour, eggs and milk; the batter is baked in the oven and is usually served with gravy.

Toad in the Hole – This is similar to Yorkshire pudding except that sausages are placed in the batter before baking.

Fish and Chips – This dish generally consists of white fish fried in flour batter and served with fried potatoes dressed in malt vinegar. Instead of ordering this "to go," as you might in America, Brits call this "take away" food.

Ploughman's Lunch – This dish, consisting of a piece of cheese, a bit of pickle, pickled onion and a chunk of bread, is most often served in pubs.

Shepherd's Pie – This dish is most often made with minced lamb and vegetables topped with a layer of mashed potatoes.

Bubble and Squeak – Typically made from cold vegetables that have been left over from a previous meal, the chief ingredients of this dish are potato and cabbage. Leftover roast meat, carrots, peas and brussels sprouts can be added. The cold chopped vegetables and meat are fried in a pan together with mashed potatoes until the mixture is well-cooked and brown on the sides. The name is a description of the action and sound made during the cooking process.

Bangers and Mash – This is, very simply, sausages and mashed potatoes. Sausages were nicknamed bangers because during wartime rationing they were so filled with water they often exploded when they were cooked.

Black Pudding – Also known as Blood Pudding, this food looks like black sausage. It's made from dried pigs' blood and fat and is generally eaten for breakfast.

Bakewell Tart – This popular English confection consists of a shortbread pastry crust with a layer of jam and a sponge filling made with almonds.

Bath Bun – The Bath bun is a rich, round sweet roll that has a lump of sugar baked in the bottom and more crushed sugar sprinkled on top after baking. Some variations include candied fruit peel or raisins.

Louis performs at Rockefeller Plaza on March 12, 2012, in New York City.

a grade at The Hayfield School. He later transferred to Hall Cross Comprehensive School, where he starred in several musical productions, most notably as Danny Zuko in *Grease*. His singing impressed theater-goers, but his decision to flash his naked bum while on stage? Well, that got him a weeklong suspension from school.

Disciplinary action aside, Louis has said his experience performing in *Grease* was what motivated him to try out for *The X Factor*.

He attended auditions in Manchester, England, where he sang The Plain White T's "Hey There Delilah." Peering out from behind side-swept bangs, the teen's voice was crisp and strong. His performance earned him three quick "yes" votes from the show's judges.

In the two-plus years since that audition and the subsequent formation of One Direction, Louis has gone from being the goofball next door to the goofball with an international following.

If he didn't understand the fervor of his fans before, he realized it when he broke up with longtime, hometown girlfriend Hannah Walker and began dating model Eleanor Calder. Thousands of fans took to Twitter in April 2012 to demand that he take back his ex-girlfriend.

The informal social media campaign infuriated Louis, who tweeted: "Truth of the matter is it's actually not funny in the slightest. I'm reading through some horrible tweets very ****ed off!" Needless to say, fans have not changed Louis' heart. He and Eleanor, who attends the University of Manchester in addition to modeling for the clothing store Hollister, have been dating since September 2011.

Louis acknowledged that making the relationship work while he's constantly on tour is difficult.

"It's a little daunting," he told HollywoodLife.com. "At the end of the day, if you want it to work, it will work. It just requires probably more effort. If your heart's in it, then you're not gonna mess about."

WAX TO THE MAX!

The guys in One Direction have reportedly appealed to the staff at Madam Tussauds to immortalize them in wax.

Madame Tussauds is a tourist attraction featuring celebrity wax figures with museums in more than a dozen cities, including London, New York, Washington, Las Vegas, Amsterdam, Berlin and Shanghai.

Don't buy your tickets just yet, though. Even if the museum decides to recreate the musicians' likenesses in wax, each life-size statue will take four months to hand craft.

Louis performs live on stage at the Hordern Pavilion on April 13, 2012, in Sydney, Australia.

Chapter 7:
LOUIS THE PRANKSTER

As serious as he is about love, Louis proudly serves as the band's comic relief. All the boys are a bit cheeky, but Louis is the biggest prankster. He is always cracking jokes and making fans laugh, especially in 1D's video diaries.

When band mate Harry falls asleep, Louis loves to turn him into a walrus by shoving straws up his nose. He's poured warm water over Zayn's hand while he was sleeping in an attempt to make him wet himself. His piggy-back riding antics are a constant distraction as the rest of the 1Ders try to sing. Some highlights among his many memorable stunts:

- In November 2010, he left the set of *The X Factor* wearing a hospital gown, purposely tucked in to expose his star-covered underpants. The sight was enough to send hordes of screaming fans into a meltdown.
- Intentional or not, Louis made headlines in 2010 when he and Harry unwittingly revealed *X Factor* winner Matt Cardle's personal mobile phone number to 7,000 fans on Twitcam. The guys decided to prank call Matt but it went straight to voicemail – which read his number out loud.
- "Can't believe I'm going to be a dad! Wow!" was the message Louis tweeted to fans on April 1, 2012. Much to the relief of his fans, it was a grand April Fools' Day prank.
- During Week 1 of *The X Factor*, Louis told the audience he was attracted to girls who ate carrots. He's not. He just thought it would be "quirky and funny." The joke's been on him, though, because girls often attend concerts dressed as carrots or wearing carrot shirts. He's also been pelted with carrots, gifted carrots and served carrots.
- In July 2012, Louis and Zayn conspired to pull a prank on their band mates. The duo hired an actress who posed as a pregnant producer from Nickelodeon. When the actress pretended to go into labor during her meeting with the group, Niall, Harry and Liam officially freaked out.

LOVE IS IN THE AIR

The candles are lit, a fire is roaring and you're on the sofa with your special someone. What's the only thing that could make the evening more romantic? A really great love song. When quizzed about his favorite romantic song, Louis named The Fray's "Look After You," which includes the lyrics:

It's always have and never hold
You've begun to feel like home
What's mine is yours to leave or take
What's mine is yours to make your own

Not a bad selection, Louis!

Louis performs at VEVO LIFT Presents One Direction Live at the EL Rey Theatre on April 1, 2012.

Chapter 7:
LOUIS THE PRANKSTER

As much grief as he sometimes gives the rest of the guys, Louis cherishes his role as a member of One Direction and says he's not sure he could handle life as a soloist.

"I don't know if me personally if I'd be able to hack it if I was a solo artist - it's a lot of time away from home," he told Radio Live New Zealand in May 2012. "But to have the other guys there with you is really nice and makes everything so much more fun."

And fun for their fans, too.

Louis performs at the Brisbane Convention and Exhibition Centre on April 18, 2012, in Australia.

Louis attends a CD signing for *Up All Night* at Walmart on March 17, 2012, in Somerdale, New Jersey.

Chapter 8:

DIRECTIONERS' DELIGHT

Chapter 8:
DIRECTIONERS' DELIGHT

Harmonies. Humor. Hair. The guys of One Direction have it all – including hoards of fans.

One Directioners, as 1D fans are known, are a loyal, enthusiastic, CD-buying, music-downloading, banner-waving, ear-splittingly loud group.

"It's Biebermania multiplied by five," said *(London) Daily Mail* writer Leah McDonald. It's true: One Direction Infection is spreading around the world at record pace.

The group's fans cover a broad spectrum of ages, but it's their youngest fans who are generally the most vocal. During the band's March 2012 visit to New York City, Louis Tomlinson teased a group of screaming girls who chased the group's bus down a busy street. When they caught up with the vehicle at a stoplight, the mob banged on its windows and rocked it from side to side.

When the light turned green, the bus was able to get away from the hysterical crowd – but not before giving the band a good scare (and earning Louis a lecture from 1D's security team.)

Ireland, England, Scotland, Australia, Canada – One Direction has fans all over the globe. But, when it comes to volume, the pop stars say their U.S. fans are among the loudest.

More than 10,000 screaming fans showed up for 1D's first American television concert in March 2012. In Nashville, dozens of girls chased the band's car down Music Row. In Natick, Mass., fans flocked to a mall when the guys held an autograph session there. And more than 100 security guards had to be hired to protect the guys

MORE DIFFERENT THAN ALIKE

The Wanted and One Direction are both U.K.-based groups of five guys who sing. As time passes, it seems those may be the only similarities between the two bands.

The bands have had a not-always-friendly rivalry going on for a while now. The feud started when The Wanted's Max George said the 1D guys were "just faces."

For their part, 1D has played down George's comments. "We haven't seen the boys, I've only read in the press what they might have said," said Louis during a U.S. promotional tour. "But as far as where we stand I think it's all pretty silly to be honest. We are two boy bands but we actually make quite different music."

Clockwise: Zayn, Niall, Louis, Harry and Liam attend the launch of their debut single, "What Makes You Beautiful" at HMV, Oxford Street on September 11, 2011, in London, England.

Chapter 8:
DIRECTIONERS' DELIGHT

One Direction poses for a photo to promote *The X Factor* final held at The Connaught Hotel on December 9, 2010, in London, England.

when they performed a show at Dallas' Dr. Pepper Park.

"The fans over here are really loud and crazy," Niall Horan told *The (London) Daily Mirror*. "When we're in the tour bus, they start climbing all over it and smacking on the windows, trying to get in. They start chasing after us, screaming ... One girl was like an Olympic sprinter. She followed us for about five blocks to our hotel. She was unbelievably fit."

Musician Olly Murs, who spent six weeks opening shows for 1D, has his own devoted fans, but that didn't keep him from being surprised by the crowds that greeted them throughout their U.S. tour.

"It was the first time I have ever been in front of One Direction's fan base, and I have never seen anything like it," Murs told *Kent (England) Online*. "Girls were running after the buses. It was quite dangerous at times, they are insane but their response was amazing ... It was very loud."

In the short two years since One

STYLE MASTERS

The 1D guys are a stylish bunch, each selecting clothing that fits his personality.

Louis, though, may be the most consistent in terms of fashion. He loves wearing striped shirts; suspenders are another favorite.

Want to mimic his fashion flare? Dress like you own a boat. Done.

Harry, Zayn, Louis (Liam is behind Louis), and Niall perform during One Direction's concert at the St. James Theatre in Wellington, New Zealand, on April 22, 2012.

One Direction performs a matinee performance at Horden Pavilion on April 13, 2012, in Sydney, Australia. (Photo by Ryan Pierse/Getty Images)

FAMOUS FANS

Yes, 1D has millions of fans around the world, but there are also plenty of high-profile celebrities who just can't get enough of Niall, Liam, Zayn, Harry and Louis:

- Katy Perry was a guest judge on the 2010 series of *The X Factor* and has been a fan of 1D from the start. Shortly after the boys made it to the top of the U.S. charts, Katy tweeted Niall "*congratulations, you didn't let me down! xo*" – in reference to her decision to put Niall through to the boot camp stage of the show.

- Justin Bieber also took to Twitter to show his support for One Direction: "*Congrats to my dudes @onedirection for the #1 album on itunes and @thewantedmusic for the #2 on singles. We share the same queen. #Canadian*"

- It should come as no surprise that Little Mix, the British four-piece girl band that won the eighth season of *The X Factor,* is firmly planted in the One Direction camp. After all, band member Perrie Edwards has long been dating dark and handsome Zayn.

  The band told Capitalfm they'd love to collaborate with the guys.

  "I think it would be really interesting – a Little Mix and One Direction (song). Imagine what that would be like," said Little Mix member Leigh-Anne Pinnock.

- In March 2012, actress-singer Miranda Cosgrove took to Twitter to give 1D her seal of approval: "*If you haven't already, check out One Direction's new album* Up All Night! *They're in an upcoming episode of iCarly and they're all great!*"

- Olly Murs, who also got his start thanks to *The X Factor,* has been an outspoken fan of 1D, often joking that he'd like to be the group's sixth member.

- Miley Cyrus is among millions of girls and women worldwide who have become obsessed with One Direction. She's confessed to a particular interest in Zayn, admitting she has spent hours watching online videos of the singer.

- Songstress Demi Lovato, who previously dated Joe Jonas, has admitted to having a crush on Niall. Despite rumors of a romantic relationship, Demi and Niall insist they're just friends.

Chapter 8:
DIRECTIONERS' DELIGHT

Direction was formed, fans have shown their appreciation in nearly every imaginable way: wearing 1D T-shirts; carrying placards and banners; bearing gifts of food, candy, jewelry and underwear; and extending prom invitations and marriage proposals. They set up fan websites and routinely send passionate handwritten letters decorated with hearts and kisses. In all, the guys have collected thousands of flowers, stuffed animals, email addresses and phone numbers. "(Fans) read what we say then send us things we mention," Liam Payne told

ENAMORED NIALL

One Direction has plenty of fans, but there are plenty of times when the tables turn and the guys, themselves, become fans. Such was the case during the 2012 Summer Olympics, when Niall reached out to fellow Mullingar, Ireland, native John Joe Nevin. Nevin medaled as a bantamweight boxer. Niall phoned Nevin prior to his semi-final bout; the two chatted for more than an hour.

Harry, Niall, Zayn, Liam, and Louis attend the VEVO GO Show presented by Starburst on April 1, 2012, in Sun Valley, California.

Liam and Zayn during One Direction's performance at the Fox Theatre on June 1, 2012, in Detroit, Michigan.

Niall and Louis sing during One Direction's performance at the St. James Theatre on April 22, 2012, in Wellington, New Zealand.

1D DOLLS, BEACH TOWELS AND MORE!

Have you ever dreamed of holding Niall, Zayn, Liam, Harry and Louis in your arms? It's simpler now that there are doll-sized versions of the pop stars.

Toymaker Vivid Imaginations put out a line of One Direction dolls (or are they action figures?) for Christmas 2011 in the U.K. and by spring 2012, Habro had released the collection in the United States. The dolls, which measure 12 to 13 inches tall, cost $27 to $43 each and are outfitted to look just like the real thing. The Louis doll, for instance, is dressed in his trademark striped shirt and the Zayn doll is wearing a red letterman-style jacket emblazoned with the One Direction logo.

Can't decide between Harry and Niall? Buy them all and stage a doll-sized concert in your bedroom.

Dolls aren't your thing? Never fear. A wide array of 1D merchandise is now available to fans around the globe.

You can decorate your room with One Direction stickers, posters, door hangers, clocks and pillows.

The guys can go to school with you if you invest in a 1D lunch box or backpack. Prefer to take them to the pool? You can. Just get yourself a One Direction swim cover up or beach towel.

The boys' handsome mugs are also, well, mugs – plus, shirts, hoodies, key rings, bracelets, earrings, pendants, phone cases and more.

What else could their images possibly be put on? Judging by merchandise sold by other entertainers, the options are limitless.

For example, you can celebrate your birthday with a Justin Bieber piñata. British Sea Power has promotional mint cakes. There are logoed condoms for the Bloc Party fan. Metallica sells metal switch plates covers.

The oddest merchandise of all? That honor goes to the rock band KISS, long known for its face paint and flamboyant costumes. The band's image decorates a coffin. Yes, a real, dead body-holding coffin. The "Kiss Kasket" is available through the band's website for $3,299 plus shipping.

The Mirror. "I get sent loads of *Toy Story* Woody dolls because I once mentioned I liked him."

Twitter, Facebook, Tumblr and YouTube have both accelerated the group's success and ensured hundreds – sometimes thousands – of fans are outside every arena or mall or hotel they visit.

Critics have likened fans' reaction to One Direction to that of The Beatles, when that band first came to the United States in 1964. It's a comparison the 1D guys have repeatedly downplayed.

"To be compared to something that was so big in its day is amazing," Louis said. "To be our generation's Beatles ... Wow. It is hugely flattering, but I'm not

One Direction attends Nickelodeon's 25th Annual Kids Choice Awards held at Galen Center on March 31, 2012, in Los Angeles, California.

One Direction attends the premiere of the Nickelodeon TV movie *Big Time Movie* in New York. (AP Photo/Charles Sykes, file)

Liam and Louis play with fuzzy earmuffs as One Direction arrives at the 2012 Logie Awards at the Crown Palladium on April 15, 2012, in Melbourne, Australia.

One Direction attends the *Harry Potter and the Deathly Hallows: Part I* world film premiere at Odeon Leicester Square on November 11, 2010, in London, England.

THERE'S A NAME FOR THAT

Loyal One Direction fans are called Directioners. But they're hardly the only music fans with their own, special nickname.

Sometimes it starts with the artist; he uses a term once to describe his fans and – boom – it catches on. Sometimes, a nickname comes from a popular lyric. Other times, fans themselves, with their homemade signs and slogans, provide the inspiration. Whatever the origin, many musicians have nicknames for their fans. Can you match these artists to their loyal ticket-buying, song-downloading, sign-waving supporters?

1.	Adam Lambert	a.	Claymates
2.	Clay Aiken	b.	Technitions
3.	David Cook	c.	Glamberts
4.	Glee	d.	Maggots
5.	Hollywood Undead	e.	Gleeks
6.	Insane Clown Posse	f.	Lambs
7.	Janet Jackson	g.	Juggalos
8.	Justin Bieber	h.	Taylors
9.	Katy Perry	i.	Undead Army
10.	Lady Gaga	j.	Moe.rons
11.	Mariah Carey	k.	Navy
12.	Moe	l.	The Victims
13.	New Kids on the Block	m.	Little Monsters
14.	Nicki Minaj	n.	KatyCats
15.	Panic! At the Disco	o.	Fanets
16.	Rhianna	p.	Bagels
17.	Slipknot	q.	Swifties
18.	Taylor Swift	r.	Barbz and Kens
19.	Tech N9ne	s.	Beliebers
20.	Wiz Khalifa	t.	Blockheads
21.	The Killers	u.	Cookies

Answers: 1-c; 2-a; 3-u; 4-e; 5-i; 6-g; 7-o; 8-s; 9-n; 10-m; 11-f; 12-j; 13-t; 14-r; 15-p; 16-k; 17-d; 18-q; 19-b; 20-h; 21-l sure how seriously we can take it because it seems so unrealistic."

It's perhaps not entirely unrealistic. Mark Medina, program director at the Washington, D.C., radio station 99.5 FM, says he's seen dozens of pop acts come and go, but he's absolutely floored by the reception One Direction has received. When it was announced the group was stopping by his station in March 2012, fans showed up en masse – some of them a full eight days before the mini-concert. Several girls traveled 2,700 miles from San Diego to hear the lads play two songs.

He told *The Washington Post*: "I'd never seen anything like it. We had people fly from other states; we had girls trying to sneak into the building."

Devoted fan Suzanne Morgan understands that kind of adoration and devotion. She stood in line for hours in anticipation of the group's

THE RAPPER IS A WRITER

"Changed The Way You Kissed Me" rapper Example says he's keen to write a track for One Direction in the future, possibly for their upcoming second studio album.

Example wrote The Wanted's 2012 hit single "Chasing The Sun."

One Direction performs at the fourth day of the 62nd Sanremo Song Festival at the Ariston Theatre on February 17, 2012, in Italy.

One Direction performs at Nickelodeon's 25th Annual Kids' Choice Awards at Galen Center on March 31, 2012, in Los Angeles, California.

November 2011 concert in Dublin. The 14-year old said the long wait paid off.

"I got really close to Niall," she told the *(London) Sunday Mirror*. "I can't believe it. It was totally worth queuing to see them. Niall was gorgeous, he is definitely the best looking, and he smiled at me."

Similarly, 15-year-old Harleigh Nunez and her mom traveled seven hours from Louisiana to Texas for One Direction's 45-minute, general admission Dallas show.

"This is a once-in-a-lifetime thing to have this experience," Harleigh told the local NBC television station, noting that a wall in her bedroom is covered with photos of the band.

The stories go on and on. Fans camp overnight before appearances. Arena shows sell out in minutes. Girls faint. One fan even took to Tumblr to share her secret for figuring out where the guys were staying on a recent tour stop: "I matched the headboard of the bed in Liam's Twitcam to every 5 star hotel in NYC."

Niall says the band loves its loyal and loud female followers but they'd like to expand their fan base by attracting more guys to their shows.

"We want to see more boy fans, as seeing them in the crowd is cool," he told Tumblr's Storyboard project. "(Right now) it's 90 percent girls, but we want to expand our fanbase. We want all people to like us."

As much as the 1D guys love their newfound fame, they know they wouldn't have any of it without their fans.

"We're five normal lads given this massive opportunity and know that without the fans we'd be nowhere," Harry Styles told the *(London) Daily*. "We feel incredibly grateful."

One Direction travels in a luxury helicopter to Glasgow, Manchester, and London on September 11, 2011, as part of a launch of their first single, "What Makes You Beautiful."

One Direction performs at the Beacon Theatre on May 26, 2012, in New York City.

LONDON OLYMPICS 2012

There are big audiences and then there are Olympic-sized audiences.

When One Direction took part in the closing ceremonies for the 2012 Summer Olympics, they performed for a live audience of 80,000 and an estimated worldwide television audience of more than 1 billion viewers. Even Prince Harry and Kate Middleton were in the crowd, representing the British Royal Family.

The London Olympics will long be remembered for performances by Michael Phelps, Mo Farah, Missy Franklin and Gabby Douglas, but 1D turned in a gold-medal act of its own.

London didn't just have a closing ceremony at the end of 17 days of Olympic competition. Instead, the city put on a toe-tapping, sing-along, wave-your-hands-in-the-air kind of party.

The show opened with an aqua-colored set representing early early-morning rush hour in London. Soon the night was off and running, turning the arena into a full-fledged street party. That's when One Direction took to the stage singing their hit, "What Makes You Beautiful," with an army of dancers performing in the background.

The guys appeared confident throughout the song. Zayn sported a new 'do with a streak of color in the front. Harry looked dapper in his charcoal woven suit. Louis was most casual in his shirt and chinos, while Liam and Niall both looked stylish in collared shirts.

E! News applauded the band's performance,

saying: "Just by putting these five cuties on stage, the Olympic organizers could do no wrong. The boys performed just as well as the previous singers—all pros who had been in the biz for decades longer."

In the moments following their Olympic performance, the guys were quick to take to Twitter to offer their thoughts:

That was SIIIIIICCKKK!!!! tweeted Harry

OMG that was unbelievable highlight of our career and the biggest audience we will ever play to 1 billion people #ThankYouLondon2012 tweeted Niall

The closing ceremony was a monstrous production, giving 1D the opportunity to perform in the same show as acts including Madness, the Pet Shop Boys, George Michael, Annie Lennox, Ed Sheeran, Russell Brand, Fatboy Slim, the Spice Girls, Muse, members of Queen and Monty Python's Eric Idle.

As International Olympic Committee President Jacques Rogge officially declared the Games of the 30th Olympiad closed, those in attendance let out an audible sigh. With the games' flame extinguished and the handover to the next summer games host, Rio de Janeiro, official, The Who came on the stage and sang: "Don't cry. ... Don't raise your eye. There's more than teenage wasteland."

Chapter 9:

THE FUTURE IS BRIGHT

Chapter 9:
THE FUTURE IS BRIGHT

Looking into the future can be a risky business, especially when it comes to predicting the fate of One Direction, the world's most popular boy band du jour.

Who knows if fans will embrace their second CD with the zeal they did the first? Who knows if another group might supplant them? Will their record company decide they should change their sound? Will the guys be able to stand up to the pressures of nearly year-round touring?

With all these unknowns, the guys say there are there two things about which they are absolutely confident:

1) Their second CD is in the works and scheduled for release in late 2012. (The first single from the new project, "Heartbreaker," produced by Carl Falk, Rami Yacoub and Savan Kotecha, has already been leaked.)

2) They are committed to sticking together. No solo acts for these guys – not in the near future, at least.

Beyond those certainties, no one – not even Niall, Liam, Harry, Zayn or Louis – knows how high their star will climb. And that's OK. The guys, it seems, are content to enjoy the fame that's been thrust upon them and see where this fast-moving train takes them.

"Performing is just incredible, when you get out of that stage and you take a moment to realize that some of the banners there are for you," Louis Payne tells *USA Today*. "It's your name on the banner, and they're shouting your name when you sing. That's still so surreal, but amazing."

Amazing? For sure. One Direction has been featured on dozens of magazine covers, made countless TV appearances, produced a behind-the-scenes book, starred in their own road movie, produced a calendar, and sold out arena concerts on three continents.

As is customary with artists just starting out their careers, One Direction members have been forced to place their trust in their management team. The guys are told where to go, when to eat, when to sleep, what to say in media interviews, even how many autographs to sign. Liam Payne says giving up that kind of control isn't difficult because – at least to this point

RED-CHEEKED

Think that embarrassing things don't happen to famous folks? You'd be wrong – very wrong – and you don't even need to look very hard to find examples.

Niall Horan, for instance, ripped the seat of his pants when he was out golfing with pal Marvin Humes in August 2012. That's right. He bent down to tie his shoe on the first hole and ... RIP!

Niall just laughed it off and powered his way around the rest of the course.

Harry performs live on stage at Hordern Pavilion on April 13, 2012, in Sydney, Australia.

ADVICE – GETTING IT AND GIVING IT

There is something about advice – people love to give it and we all get it, whether we want it or not.

The One Direction guys are in a position to receive lots of advice these days; we suspect not all of it is solicited, but they're nice guys, so they smile and listen. Here's a sampling of some of the most public advice they've received of late:

Actor/singer **Zac Efron**, who skyrocketed to fame in Disney's *High School Musical*: "Realize there's more to life than being famous. If you start to believe your own hype and get carried away, you won't last in the industry."

Howie Dorough, who performed with The Backstreet Boys: "Get a good lawyer! Get your contracts checked!"

N'Sync band member **Joey Fatone**: "It's every 15 year old's dream to be rich and famous and tour the world and be in a band - and it is cool. But you're not going to have a girlfriend, you're not going to finish school, you're not going to your prom ... you're going to miss all of those experiences in life. There's a reason we go through all that stuff and when you miss out on that, it's going to cost and later in life you're going to have to make up for that stuff, slowly over a long period of time, or you shut down for a few years. It's going to show up."

Aaron Carter, 1990s pop and hip hop singer via Twitter to the band: "You guys are dope ... don't go getting' corny and sh*t!! Listen to your manager!"

N'SYNC member **Lance Bass** upon hearing that Harry Styles had rented a $195,000 Ferrari: "Save your money! Save your money! Invest in something that will make you money. Trust me."

English singer-songwriter **Elton John**: "If I had to give them advice I would say to keep your original friends, keep good counsel with them."

Backstreet Boys member **AJ McLean**: "My best advice is, 'Don't ask for advice.'"

Of course, giving often brings more joy than receiving, so the guys have been sure to share sage advice with others. Here are a few of their bits of wisdom, specifically intended for those thinking about auditioning for a show like *The X Factor*:

Liam Payne: "I think the best advice we can give to anybody who's auditioning for *X Factor* is just to go out there and have fun. Kind of separate yourself from everybody else. Do something that makes you a little bit different. And kind of put yourself out there."

Louis Tomlinson: "Don't let your nerves get to you ... Get over it really quick because it might catch up with you later on."

Niall Horan: "Just enjoy it, I think. A lot of people, because it's so intense, might kind of let it all close in on them, and they might get overwhelmed. But you just need to enjoy it for what it is and just have fun with it."

Harry Styles: "Just rehearse, rehearse, rehearse as well. You can't rehearse enough for the audition."

Zayn performs at HMV Hammersmith Apollo on January 22, 2012, in London, England.

Chapter 9:
THE FUTURE IS BRIGHT

– the guidance they're getting seems to be working.

On July 31, 2012, 1D was presented with special discs by Syco Music and Sony Music in the United Kingdom for having 12 million in worldwide sales in less than a year. According to Sony Music, One Direction's sales to that date included 8 million singles, 3 million albums and 1 million DVDs.

WHAT'S IN THAT CARE PACKAGE?

Like most growing boys, the 1D guys love to eat. Among their favorite snacks? Treats made by Zayn Malik's mother. "I love samosas filled with mincemeat," he said. "My mum makes really great ones." (Samosas are traditional sweet Indian sundries.) "Zayn's mum makes such great food," agreed band mate Niall Horan. "I can eat so much."

Even as the band's debut CD continued to fly off the shelves, they happily headed to the studio to record their second album.

Niall Horan told the *National Post* that the group began meeting with songwriters and producers in spring 2012.

"We want to bring out a

Niall and Liam travel with their One Direction band mates in a luxury helicopter to Glasgow, Manchester, and London on September 11, 2011, to launch their first single, "What Makes You Beautiful."

Niall performs at HMV Hammersmith Apollo on January 22, 2012, in London, England.

TWO BANDS, ONE NAME

It appears One Direction may actually be Two.

In April 2012, an American band claiming to be the original One Direction sued Sony Music and Syco Entertainment for $1 million, charging that the U.K. band is confusing fans and ruining the credibility of the U.S. group.

Documents filed in the U.S. District Court in California allege that the U.K's One Direction learned they shared the name when they attempted to file with the U.S. Trademark Office.

"We were negotiating for about a month before we filed the complaint," the plaintiffs' lawyer, Peter Ross, told E! News. "In our view, negotiations had stalled and weren't going anywhere."

The one thing the two groups agree on: that they can't agree.

A spokesman for the U.K.-based One Direction said in a statement: "There is a dispute with a local group in California about the ownership of the One Direction name in the U.S.

"One Direction's management tried to resolve the situation amicably when the matter first came to light, but the Californian group has now filed a lawsuit claiming they own the name. One Direction's lawyers now have no choice but to defend the lawsuit and the band's right to use their name."

The battle of the band names intensified in June 2012, when chart-topping boy band One Direction filed a countersuit against California's One Direction, alleging they actually had their name swiped by the U.S. group.

A statement from the better known One Direction reads: "One Direction's lawyers have now had to file an Answer and Counterclaim in order to defend and assert the band's right to use their name. The Answer and Counterclaim makes it clear that it is One Direction who has prior rights to the name in the U.S., as it was One Direction who used the name in interstate commerce in the U.S. first."

The U.S. version of One Direction is fronted by Sean O'Leary. The pop group is not signed to a label but has been selling its album, *The Light*, on iTunes since February 2011. The Harry-Liam-Niall-Louis- Zayn- version of One Direction became the first U.K. band to debut at No. 1 on the Billboard 200 with their first U.S. album, *Up All Night*.

While lawyers continue to arm wrestle over name rights, it's good to note this is hardly the first time two bands have gone to war over a name – a few memorable battles:

- Two bands – one a group of young heart-throbs, the other a trio of Scottish 50-somethings – settled a 2003 court dispute with the agreement that both would continue to call themselves Blue.
- In 2005, Scottish indie rockers Eskimo Blonde demanded that a girl

trio who found sudden fame on *The X Factor* change its name. The dispute was quickly resolved when the Liverpool girl group was eliminated from the televised talent show.

- Rock band Pink Floyd has endured several name changes. One of the group's earliest names was Tea Set – until they found themselves playing in a big show with another band with the same name.
- The Grateful Dead was once known as The Warlocks but was forced to change its name when another band called The Warlocks landed a record deal. Meanwhile, a third Warlocks group was playing up and down the East Coast. That band became Velvet Underground.
- George Michael and Andrew Ridgeley were a 1980s British duo called Wham! For a short time, the band was known in the United States as Wham! UK due to a name conflict with a lesser known American band.

Chapter 9:
THE FUTURE IS BRIGHT

Left to right: Niall, Harry, Zayn, Liam, and Louis pose for photographs while visiting Glasgow, Manchester, and London on September 11, 2011. (Photo by Dave Hogan/Getty Images)

record nearly every year, every year and a half," he said.

The guys are determined that future projects will reflect their own, personal music tastes. Niall, for example, prefers The Script and singer-songwriter Ed Sheeran. Harry's musical tastes lean toward Foster the People, Coldplay and Kings of Leon.

"We want to have a little bit heavier guitars, bigger drums, more of a live feel, because that's what we like doing," said Harry, insisting fans shouldn't worry about the group moving away from its pop roots and into the grunge scene. "...It's important that we like what we're doing as well," said Harry. "It wouldn't be good if we

THIS TEAM BROUGHT TO YOU BY LOUIS

Louis Tomlinson bought a football team? No, not really. The Three Horse Shoes team in Doncaster, England, wasn't actually for sale. But the amateur footballers needed new uniforms and, since Louis used to play for the team, he was happy to help out. His one stipulation – he'd like the chance to play on the team if One Direction's busy touring schedule ever allows it.

Louis performs at HMV Hammersmith Apollo on January 22, 2012, in London, England.

weren't enjoying what we're doing – and we are."

There's been lots of talk – by the guys themselves, reporters and other musicians and songwriters – about partnering on future projects. Ed Sheeran, Paul McCartney, Justin Bieber, Labrinth, Big Time Rush, Rihanna, Katy Perry, Taylor Swift and Jennifer Lopez are among the many artists who have been listed as possible collaborators.

Whether or not any of these team projects end up on band's second album, the boys have made no secret of the fact that they're excited about it. Need proof? Check out these tweets:

Harry, on June 22, 2012: "*Can't wait to finish this album and for you guys to hear it... hope you like it! X.*"

Niall, on July 27, 2012: "*In the studio recording guitar with @carlfalkmusic! Next year's tour is gonna be fun ! #liveguitar.*"

Niall on July 28, 2012: "*What a sick day in the studio! Got loads of vocal down and recorded 2 songs! On guitar! #worldtour2013 #cantwait.*"

Liam on July 27, 2012: "*Studio was amazing today. Can't wait for the new album to be readdyyy.*"

Liam on Aug. 8, 2012: "*I can't wait for you guys to hear the new albummm !!!*"

Almost as soon as the new album is completed, the guys will hit the road for their first worldwide tour – with very few nights off along the way. They acknowledge it's a hectic schedule, but they're anxious to show fans that they're much more than a one-hit (or one-CD) wonder.

And, for all those rumor-mongers who say

Left to right: Zayn, Liam, Louis, and Niall perform live on stage at Trusts Stadium on April 21, 2012, in Auckland, New Zealand.

Liam performs at Liverpool Echo Arena on January 15, 2012, in England.

Chapter 9:
THE FUTURE IS BRIGHT

the band will soon disband. The guys say they're in it for the long haul.

In a July 2012 interview with *The (London) Sun*, Liam said he's opposed to the notion of going solo. "I think it would be massively, massively boring! I don't know how Justin Bieber does it, but full props to him. I like being around the boys. I enjoy other people's company, and it's a lot more fun being in a band on stage."

Fans couldn't agree more. One pop star is good. Five pop stars on one stage, working as One Direction is beyond dreamy.

Louis, Niall, Harry, Liam, and Zayn perform at HMV Hammersmith Apollo on January 22, 2012, in London, England.

One Direction performs at Nickelodeon's 25th Annual Kids' Choice Awards held at Galen Center on March 31, 2012, in Los Angeles, California.

2013 ONE DIRECTION WORLD TOUR DATES

Feb. 22, 2013........................The O2 Arena, London, England
Feb. 23, 2013........................The O2 Arena, London, England
Feb. 24, 2013........................The O2 Arena, London, England
Feb. 25, 2013........................Scottish Exhibition and Conference Centre, Glasgow, Scotland
Feb. 26, 2013........................Scottish Exhibition and Conference Centre, Glasgow, Scotland
March 1, 2013......................Motorpoint Arena, Cardiff, Wales
March 2, 2013......................Motorpoint Arena, Cardiff, Wales
March 5, 2013......................The O2, Dublin, Ireland
March 6, 2013......................The O2, Dublin, Ireland
March 7, 2013......................Odyssey Arena, Belfast, Northern Ireland
March 8, 2013......................Odyssey Arena, Belfast, Northern Ireland
March 10, 2013....................Odyssey Arena, Belfast, Northern Ireland
March 11, 2013.....................Odyssey Arena, Belfast, Northern Ireland
March 12, 2013....................The O2, Dublin, Ireland
March 13, 2013....................The O2, Dublin, Ireland
March 15, 2013....................Manchester Arena, Manchester, England
March 16, 2013....................Manchester Arena, Manchester, England
March 17, 2013....................Echo Arena Liverpool, Liverpool, England
March 19, 2013....................Motorpoint Arena, Sheffield, England
March 20, 2013...................Capital FM Arena, Nottingham, England
March 22, 2013...................LG Arena, Birmingham, England
March 23, 2013...................LG Arena, Birmingham, England
March 31, 2013....................Echo Arena, Liverpool, England
April 1, 2013..........................The O2 Arena, London, England
April 2, 2013.........................The O2 Arena, London, England
April 4, 2013.........................The O2 Arena, London, England
April 5, 2013.........................The O2 Arena, London, England
April 8, 2013.........................Metro Radio Arena, Newcastle, England
April 9, 2013.........................Metro Radio Arena, Newcastle, England
April 12, 2013.......................Scottish Exhibition and Conference Centre, Glasgow, Scotland
April 13, 2013.......................Motorpoint Arena, Sheffield, England
April 14, 2013.......................Motorpoint Arena, Sheffield, England

April 17, 2013........................LG Arena, Birmingham, England
April 19, 2013........................Manchester Arena, Manchester, England
June 13, 2013........................Bank Atlantic Center, Fort Lauderdale, FL
June 14, 2013........................American Airlines Arena, Miami, FL
June 16, 2013........................KFC Yum! Center, Louisville, KY
June 18, 2013........................Nationwide Arena, Columbus, OH
June 19, 2013........................Bridgestone Arena, Nashville, TN
June 21, 2013........................Philips Arena, Atlanta, GA
June 22, 2013........................RBC Center, Raleigh, NC
June 23, 2013........................Verizon Center, Washington, DC
June 25, 2013........................Wells Fargo Center, Philadelphia, PA
June 26, 2013........................Comcast Center, Mansfield, MA
June 28, 2013........................Nikon at Jones Beach Theater, Wantagh, NY
June 29, 2013........................Nikon at Jones Beach Theater, Wantagh, NY
July 2, 2013........................Izod Center, East Rutherford, NJ
July 4, 2013........................Bell Centre, Montreal, QC
July 5, 2013........................Hersheypark Stadium, Hershey, PA
July 6, 2013........................Hersheypark Stadium, Hershey, PA
July 8, 2013........................Consol Energy Center, Pittsburgh, PA
July 9, 2013........................Air Canada Centre, Toronto, ON
July 10, 2013........................Air Canada Centre, Toronto, ON
Jul. 12, 2013........................Palace Of Auburn Hills, Auburn Hills, MI
July 13, 2013........................First Midwest Bank Amphitheatre, Tinley Park, IL
July 14, 2013........................First Midwest Bank Amphitheatre, Tinley Park, IL
July 18, 2013........................Target Center, Minneapolis, MN
July 19, 2013........................Sprint Center, Kansas City, MO
July 21, 2013........................Toyota Center, Houston, TX
July 22, 2013........................American Airlines Center, Dallas, TX
July 24, 2013........................Pepsi Center, Denver, CO
July 25, 2013........................Maverik Center, Salt Lake City, UT
July 27, 2013........................Rogers Arena, Vancouver, BC
July 28, 2013........................Key Arena, Seattle, WA
July 30, 2013........................HP Pavilion, San Jose, CA
July 31, 2013........................ORACLE Arena, Oakland, CA
Aug. 2, 2013........................Mandalay Bay Events Center, Las Vegas, NV
Aug. 3, 2013........................Mandalay Bay Events Center, Las Vegas, NV
Aug. 6, 2013........................Cricket Wireless Amphitheatre, Chula Vista, CA
Aug. 7, 2013........................Staples Center, Los Angeles, CA
Aug. 8, 2013........................Staples Center, Los Angeles, CA

CINEMAS DECEMBER
SPONSORED BY
Sky 3D

One Direction performs at Nickelodeon's 25th Annual Kids' Choice Awards held at Galen Center on March 31.